COOKing
FOR
BUSY MUMS

AMANDA VOISEY

Cooking for busy mums

Fast, fresh and family-friendly meals

First published in 2016

Copyright © Amanda Voisey 2016

Allen & Unwin
83 Alexander Street
Crows Nest NSW 2065
Australia
Phone: (61 2) 8425 0100
Email: info@allenandunwin.com
Web: www.allenandunwin.com

Cataloguing-in-Publication details are available
from the National Library of Australia
www.trove.nla.gov.au

ISBN 978 1 76029 224 9

Internal design by Christa Moffit, Christabella Designs
Index by Puddingburn Publishing Services
Set in 12/17 pt Gill Sans by Midland Typesetters, Australia
Printed and bound in Australia by Griffin Press

10 9 8 7 6 5 4 3 2 1

MIX
Paper from
responsible sources
FSC® C009448
www.fsc.org

The paper in this book is FSC® certified. FSC® promotes environmentally responsible, socially beneficial and economically viable management of the world's forests.

I dedicate this book to my husband, Luke, and my sons, Rhylee and Liam, who made me a mum; and to my family who have always encouraged me to do what I love. Also thank you for being my taste testers.

contents

The Beginning

In September of 2009 I became a mum: it was the best day of my life. My son was finally in my arms after a mammoth labour and we were now a family.

To say becoming a mum changed my life is an understatement. You are never really prepared for how much a little bundle of joy will change the way you do everything that you used to do pre-baby.

I can sit here now laughing at the memories of shovelling dinners into my mouth so fast that they didn't even get a chance to hit my tastebuds; snacking on muesli bars and the like during baby's feeding time, as I was starving and had no time to stop and cook something decent to eat. The first few months were hard and I knew I had to change the way I approached our meals, as the current way wasn't working.

One morning I was feeding my son, who was now four months old, in front of the computer (he used to feed for so long). I had recently joined Facebook and was scrolling through my newsfeed when I noticed that you could create a page to share something you were passionate about with like-minded people all over the world. My current situation was that I was a busy mum, I knew how to cook (I had worked in the food industry since my first job at fourteen years old and went on to fulfil a dream of owning a cafe while completing my university studies), but I was struggling to put the two together in my new life. As my son finished his feed, I was burping him, taking in my current thoughts. When I finished I placed him in his rocker beside me while I seized the moment to make a Facebook page.

Cooking for Busy Mums was born, but what was I thinking? I didn't have time for this. I had made a page on Facebook, found an image of a woman with a chef's hat on and used that as my profile photo, then invited my friends to like the page and started to share new quick dinner ideas and the like. To my amazement, the page grew by a thousand 'likes' a day: I couldn't believe it. I quickly learnt that Facebook made it hard to keep track of recipes and photos so I did some searching and discovered something called a blog (again, this was all very new to me more than six years ago).

I created the blog, gave myself a crash course in how to use it and started to post recipes and photos (that weren't very good, when I look back at the earlier recipes). I added the link to the recipes on my Facebook page and, well, the rest is history. Today I have two sons who make my life busier, yet more fulfilling, than ever before and Cooking For Busy Mums has grown to a following of more than 615 000 Facebook fans, the website <www.cookingforbusymums. com> has an average 250 000 page views a month, and there is an awesome, continually growing community on Instagram.

Every week I have continued to share new recipes that we have eaten as a family so my community can enjoy them in their homes too.

Along this journey I have been very lucky to have the support of long-term sponsors (Kambrook, D'Orsogna and Dairy Australia, to name a few) that have helped me continue my work and also open up a whole range of new meals for the community to try.

Putting together the most popular recipes from the blog and adding fantastic new ones to create this cookbook has been something I have wanted to do for such a long time (and I can't believe it is here). This is a resource that will allow you to cook your family real food that is made from everyday ingredients (except, perhaps, for chia seeds, which I simply love) that are fresh and family friendly, and that don't require complex steps to make.

My meals are focused around making sure you are providing a well-balanced meal at breakfast, lunch and dinner with minimal effort, and using ingredients that are budget-friendly and likely to be eaten by all the members of the family.

Using these easy recipes, you will begin to enjoy cooking again; or, if you aren't much of a cook, you will be able to begin your cooking journey.

In addition to the recipes, I have included extra resources to broaden your food knowledge and provide tips that will be useful in your home.

In this book, you will find:

- information on family nutrition from Mandy at Little People Nutrition (as well as advice based on my experiences with fussy eating and how we work with it),
- which kitchen appliances make my life easier, as my extra helping hands in the kitchen,
- tips to save you money at the supermarket, starting with your very next shopping trip,
- a list of pantry staples, the everyday ingredients you should always have in your pantry, fridge and freezer to make meal times easier, and
- ideas about packing a school lunchbox.

So jump in, mark your favourite recipes and get cooking.

Getting Started

symbols used in this book

For ease of reference, you will notice icons like these used with each recipe. These are there to let you know how to store the meal once it is cooked.

FRIDGE

This means that once the meal is cooked it can be stored in an airtight container in the fridge for up to three days. It also means that this meal is great for leftovers that can be reheated in either a microwave or oven (if it is a hot meal) and enjoyed for lunch the next day or dinner within three days of cooking.

If it is a sweet item (such as muffins, biscuits (cookies) or slices, store them in an airtight container and they will last between five and seven days.

FREEZER

This means that once the meal is cooked it can be cooled and stored in a freezer-safe container (I like to use resealable plastic bags) and kept in the freezer for up to three months.

When ready to eat, remove from the freezer and leave to thaw in the fridge before reheating (if a hot meal) in the microwave or oven.

If it is a sweet item (such as muffins, biscuits (cookies) or slices) I store these individually in resealable plastic bags and put them straight into my sons' lunchboxes. They are thawed by morning tea time.

PANTRY

You will find this symbol with pantry-stable items such as biscuits. These can be stored in an airtight container in a cupboard or cool, dark place for up to one week.

LEFTOVERS

This means that the meal you have cooked can be eaten the next day (and up to three days from cooking) for lunch or dinner. Depending on the meal simply reheat to serve or enjoy as is.

Measurements

The measurements used for ingredients throughout this book are Australian and New Zealand metric.

METRIC CUPS AND SPOONS (LIQUIDS)

1 cup	250 ml	9 fl oz
¾ cup	185 ml	6 fl oz
⅔ cup	170 ml	5½ fl oz
½ cup	125 ml	4 fl oz
⅓ cup	80 ml	2½ fl oz
¼ cup	60 ml	2 fl oz
1 tablespoon	20 ml	½ fl oz
1 teaspoon	5 ml	³⁄₁₆ fl oz

For dry ingredients here are some common weights of 1 cup of ingredients.

Plain (all-purpose) or self-raising flour	150 g	5½ oz
White sugar, caster (superfine) sugar	220 g	7¾ oz
Brown sugar, lightly packed	185 g	6½ oz
Icing (confectioners') sugar	125 g	4½ oz
Honey	350 g	12 oz
Golden syrup (light treacle)	350 g	12 oz
Desiccated (dried shredded) coconut	90 g	3¼ oz
Rolled (porridge) oats	95 g	3¼ oz
Sultanas (golden raisins)	170 g	6 oz
Dates (chopped)	160 g	5¾ oz
Cornflakes	30 g	1 oz
Rice Bubbles (puffed rice)	25 g	1 oz
Breadcrumbs (dry)	110 g	3¾ oz
Breadcrumbs (fresh)	60 g	2¼ oz
Grated cheese (cheddar, tasty, parmesan)	100 g	3½ oz
Rice	200 g	7 oz
Couscous	190 g	6¾ oz

EGGS

The quantity of eggs for a recipe is based on 70 g (Grade 3) eggs unless otherwise specified.

OVEN TEMPERATURES

Temperatures recommended for all recipes cooked in the oven are for an electric fan-forced oven. If you are using a conventional oven, increase the temperature by 20°C (35°F).

Balanced Family Nutrition

BY MANDY DOS SANTOS

My resident nutritionist and mum of three, Mandy from Little People Nutrition, shares with us the importance of a balanced family diet.

To encourage balanced and healthy family nutrition, we must focus on how we eat as much as what we eat. The combination of nurturing positive eating habits and developing our children's conscious and subconscious food choices will benefit them as they learn to make their own decision as adults and for their own families.

Before we delve into why we eat certain foods or food groups it is helpful to highlight some simple tools to aid you in making better choices for your family, even when you are busy and flustered.

Firstly, cooking your own meals is one of the most fundamental healthy eating habits you can establish as a parent, even if it is simply eggs on toast or fruit salad and yoghurt. These are far better options then processed foods that are high in sugar and salt, often delivered to your door. When cooking your own meals you are more likely to choose whole unprocessed foods that are devoid of preservatives, artificial additives and ingredients. Your children will also better understand where their food comes from and how to cook it.

Secondly, sitting down to eat as a family is the ultimate way to inspire children to eat their meal while modelling good eating habits. Eating the same meal is even better. Eating together as a family encourages positive social interaction and is also strongly associated with mental and emotional wellbeing for all family members, especially children.

Thirdly, three very basic nutrition principles will guide you when you are under pressure or tired:

1. Choose unprocessed fresh foods first.
2. Plant-based foods, such as vegetables, should make up the majority of your plate (even in each meal or snack if you can).
3. Variety, variety, variety. Choose different vegetables, different fruits, different grain options, different protein sources. The more variety throughout the day, week and month, the wider and greater the source of nutrition. Simply eat a rainbow.

And now to delve deeper into food groups. The Australian Dietary Guidelines are an effective, simple and informative tool to guide what, and how much, we should be aspiring to cook and prepare for our families. The guidelines divide food into five main groups, which are:

- vegetables,
- fruits,
- grains and cereals,
- lean meats, poultry, seafood, tofu, eggs, nuts, seeds and legumes, and
- dairy and calcium-rich alternatives.

Each section of the population has different recommended serving guidelines. To simplify it we will focus on non-pregnant and non-lactating women, and children who are around five years old.

VEGETABLES

Vegetables include green leafy vegies, such as spinach, bok choy (pak choy), silverbeet (Swiss chard), all the way to potatoes and even legumes such as peas, chickpeas (garbanzo beans) and navy beans. Vegetables are the true superfoods.

Only 6 per cent of the Australian population consumes adequate vegetables each day, yet they are probably the most important determinant of our families' health and are associated with the prevention of non-communicable diseases such as cardiovascular disease and type 2 diabetes, which are prevalent in our society.

The reasons why vegies are an important choice are infinite. Vitamins, minerals, phytochemicals, antioxidants, fibre and water are just a few of the nutrients they contain. Adults should consume five serves of vegies a day and a five-year-old child should be consuming 4½ serves.

How much is a serve? It is the same for all ages across the food groups. For vegetables, a serve is 75 g (2¾ oz) or ½ cup of cooked vegetables or 1 cup (about 40 g/ 1 ½ oz) of raw salad.

One of the simplest ways to increase your vegetable intake is to think about simply adding more at each meal. Spinach with eggs for breakfast (cooked, or in a smoothie), fresh vegetable sticks at morning tea or crunch and sip break for the kids; grated vegetables in a sandwich for the kids and a side salad with your lunch; by dinner time you only need to add a few more serves.

FRUIT

Fruit is packed full of energy, vitamins, minerals, antioxidants and phytochemicals as well as fibre, and if we eat it in its purest form, we will be on our way to a healthy diet.

Sadly, once they reach school age, many children reduce their intake of whole fruits as fruit juice starts to creep into their diet. Eating whole, unprocessed fruit is in line with the first two of the simple eating principles (wholefoods and plant-based) and children around five years should be aiming for 1 ½ serves a day (for adults, 2 serves a day).

A few tips to keep in mind when eating fruit is to watch out for processed fruit in the form of gels, slurries or even disguised 'fruit foods'. If you are going to choose canned options, aim for fruit in juice rather than in syrup. Frozen fruits are also a great way to eat fruit and add them to smoothies, baked treats or even yoghurt. If you intend on eating the fibre-rich skin of fresh fruits, ensure you wash it well before eating and, to be extra careful, you could even soak them in vinegar and water in your sink before popping them in the fridge or in the fruit bowl.

CEREALS AND GRAINS

When we talk about cereals and grains, people often think solely of wheat-based pasta and bread. Although delicious and incredibly nutritious, there are many other grain and cereal options and, remembering the simple nutrition principles, variety is best.

Rice, quinoa, spelt, rye, wheat, corn and oats are the basis of different kinds of dishes and foods such as pasta, puffed cereals, noodles or breads, to name a few. These grains and cereals provide a nutrient-dense carbohydrate source, which is important for energy and digestive and heart health; they also offer essential nutrients such as iron and folate. It is advised to choose wholegrain varieties that are less processed to get the greater benefit from this food group. If you are gluten-sensitive or coeliac, grains such as rice, quinoa, corn and sometimes spelt and oats provide a gluten-free or low-grain option. See a doctor for advice.

Although the dietary guidelines talk about 6 serves for female adults and 4 serves for children, scope out what a serve actually comprises: you will be surprised how small it is. One slice of bread is a serve or ½ cup of cooked pasta or rice or alternative grain. Measure it out and see the size: six serves no longer seems like a lot!

LEAN PROTEIN AND ALTERNATIVES

Protein comes in many forms, from meat to lentils and even dairy sources. In Australia we are very lucky to have an abundance of meat proteins such as beef, lamb, poultry and seafood. In fact, our nation is slightly obsessed with protein. Although it is incredibly important in our diets for both adults and children, we need to be mindful that again whole fresh sources are best; additional powders and supplementation are not necessary for our health, if we are otherwise well.

Protein is key for cell renewal and growth and that is why it is crucial for growth in children as well as immunity. High-protein foods are also great providers of important minerals and vitamins such as vitamin B12, iron, zinc and essential fatty acids.

We should be aiming for around 2½ serves of protein a day as adults and 1½ serves for a five year old. A serving size is 65 g (2½ oz) for cooked lean red meat, 80 g (2¾ oz) for cooked poultry, 100 g (3½ oz) for cooked fish, 2 large eggs, 1 cup (200 g/7 oz) of cooked or canned legumes and 30 g (1 oz) of nuts.

Remember that those serves of protein do not all have to come from lean meat sources: fatty fish, seafood, nuts, eggs and legumes are equally important sources of these vitamins and minerals. Eating a variety of proteins is key to our health, as well as the health of our environment.

DAIRY

Dairy and alternative calcium-rich sources are important for all the family but probably most of all for children and women, helping with the development of strong bones and the maintenance of bone health as we get older.

Children are avid consumers of dairy, in the form of milk, when they are younger but as they reach school age milk often does not feature in their diets as strongly as it once did. When girls get older, they often see dairy foods as fattening and also reduce their intake. This is distressing for many reasons, but it is crucial that children maintain their intake of approximately 2 serves per day from a variety of sources, such as milk, yoghurt and cheese. Non-dairy sources that are still calcium-rich include nuts, seeds, leafy green vegetables, tofu and salmon.

Women from 19–50 years require 2½ serves per day. Women over 50 years old are recommended to have 4 serves.

A serving size is 250 ml (9 fl oz) or 1 cup of milk, 200 g (7 oz) or ¾ cup of yoghurt and 2 slices or 40 g (1½ oz) of cheese.

If you are choosing non-dairy milks, ensure they are fortified with calcium at 100 mg of calcium per 100 ml.

Most importantly, enjoy any meal or cooking experience with your family and create memories and traditions that are special to just yourselves. Remember, food is nutrition of course, but it is also culture, language, love, history and memories.

Are they really fussy eaters?

Sometimes I would call my school-age children fantastic eaters; at other times I would call them fussy eaters, simply because they will devour meals and foods that are familiar to them and then reject new meals.

This can be frustrating for adults, as we know that trying new foods is exciting, but younger children don't share that sense of excitement. This is why we categorise them as being fussy, when really what they are saying is, 'Hold on a minute here, Mum. I don't know what this is. I have never seen it before. Why should I eat it?'

For younger children, familiarity and routine is key to keeping them happy and comfortable in their environment, so when we place a meal in front of them with foods they have never seen before they are confused and don't know what they are meant to do. We can use this understanding in the way we approach the introduction of new foods or meals. I will give you an example: in our house, we have just convinced the kids to eat orange and red foods simply by having carrot and sweet potato in many meals during the past few weeks. The boys became used to seeing carrots and sweet potato on their plate; they had tried it before, they knew that they liked the taste of it and now in their little memory bank they have good associations with carrots and sweet potatoes. At each meal I would clearly tell them what was on their plate and remind them that they had tried it before. This made them feel comfortable with the meal and willing to eat it.

Green vegetables are a bit more of a challenge, maybe because green is often likened to 'goo' or yucky things in children's books, television shows and toys. Each time we have greens I still put them on their plates, tell them what they are, ask them if they would like to:

- smell them,
- lick them, or
- have a nibble.

I'm continuing to repeat this process at mealtime after mealtime and gradually but surely we are making a positive association with green foods.

Let me recap what I have learned from my children when it comes to eating:

- They aren't fussy, they just don't like the unknown.
- Building positive associations with a wide variety of foods is essential.
- Familiarity and consistency is key: the more they see the same food, the more likely they are to eat it.
- Introduce a new meal and serve it a couple of times and don't give up when they refuse to eat it the first time they are served it.
- Finally, remember that they will grow out of it. My eldest is a whole lot more open to trying new foods now than he was a year ago.

Don't get stressed at mealtimes when they won't eat; it only makes things worse. I always tell my boys if you don't want to eat the dinner that is on the table there is nothing else to eat, so if you are hungry, you had better start eating.

Kitchen appliances that make my life easier

These days we are very lucky to have access to many kitchen appliances that make cooking easier and more efficient. For my recipes I do rely on a couple of appliances that are the workhorses in my kitchen. I have been lucky to be sponsored by Kambrook for many years now, so I have had the chance to put many appliances through their paces and decide which ones really do make a busy mum's life easier.

These are my top-rated kitchen appliances that I use on a daily basis: they don't cost an arm and a leg and I believe they are essential to making great meals and making the most of your cooking time.

FOOD PROCESSOR

This is my number one appliance. It's a little machine, but it can perform so many functions faster than I can by hand. For mixing, processing, grating, kneading and slicing, the food processor helps you get the job done. It is easy to clean and can be used for making both savoury and sweet dishes. It really is a third hand in the kitchen.

STAND MIXER

Mixing cakes, muffins, biscuits and icing (frosting) has never been easier. You keep both of your hands free to wrangle a toddler or do the dishes as it does all the mixing for you. This is essential if you love to bake sweets. It also has a kneading attachment for making bread and pizza dough.

BLENDER

I use the Blitz2Go and the BlitzPro and smoothie-making is a breeze. They can do more than smoothies as well. I use them to make dips, sauces, purées, pancake batters and whipped cream as well.

SLOW COOKER

While I am yet to convert to using a slow cooker in summer (simply because we use the barbecue a lot during the warmer weather) it is really a lifesaver for nights when you know you will be home late after work or after school activities. Look for one that can also cook rice so you can get even more use from it.

NON-STICK FRYING PAN

This is not an appliance as such, but it is a much-used item in my kitchen. Investing in a good non-stick frying pan will ensure you use less oil during cooking and your food cooks efficiently and evenly.

SHARP KNIFE

I slice and dice something nearly every day. You need a sharp, good-quality cutting knife in the kitchen to make prep time easy. There is nothing worse than a blunt knife that hacks at your food. Just remember to store it out of reach of the little ones.

10 tips to save money at the supermarket

If you feel that your food-shopping budget is blowing out most weeks, then give some or all of these tips a try. You might be surprised how much you can save without sacrificing what you eat.

1. Shop in your fridge, freezer and pantry first, before you hit the shops. By doing this you know what you have and what you need to make meals for the week.

2. Subscribe to Coles' and Woolworths' (major supermarket chains) catalogues so that it's emailed to you the day before the specials start. That way you can compare what is on sale before you leave. If you have an Aldi (budget supermarket) near you, then shop there first and top up with the missing items from the other supermarkets' sale catalogues.

3. As good as meal planning is, if you plan a meal and then find that the 'special' ingredient you need is rather expensive, you may actually start to spend more. Make sure your meal plan allows for flexibility and allows you to use everyday ingredients or use the special item in multiple meals during the week.

4. Buy seasonal only. This will save money on fruit and vegetables; for example, I don't buy strawberries when they are $5 a punnet, I buy another fruit that is seasonal and cheaper. By doing this, you also get fruit and vegetables that are at their peak and full of nutrients and flavour.

5. Make an effort to bake cakes and biscuits. Slice your own meat for stir-frying. Buy whole chickens and cut them into portions. These are just a few examples of buying

ingredients closer to their natural state, as these are always cheaper. You then make them into the item you want instead of paying for a packaging company to make them into the item you want.

6. When making your dinner meal, make enough to have leftovers that you can eat for lunch the next day. This will reduce the amount of money you spend on lunches.

7. One night a week, have a leftover night where you eat whatever's in your fridge that needs eating. Explore new ways to make another meal from leftovers such as roast meats.

8. When toiletries and cleaning products you prefer to use are on sale, buy an extra one so that when they aren't on sale you will have a back-up and avoid paying full price.

9. Don't take your partner or children shopping. They end up putting things in the trolley you don't need. Also shop on a full stomach; there is nothing worse than shopping when you're hungry, as you will buy more than you need.

10. Instead of shopping once every week, try to stretch it out to eight or nine days. By doing this you will only do a full shop three times a month instead of four. It will make you use what you already have in the fridge, freezer and pantry. This will reduce food spoilage and save money in the month.

pantry, fridge and freezer staples list

These are items that I recommend you always have on hand. They are basic items that will always allow you to cook something, even when you think you have nothing to cook with.

PANTRY
- Plain (all-purpose) and self-raising flour
- Sugar: brown and raw (unrefined)
- Baking powder
- Bicarbonate of soda (baking soda)
- Cornflour (cornstarch)
- Unsweetened cocoa powder
- Chocolate chips
- Natural vanilla essence
- Oats: rolled (porridge) and instant
- Breadcrumbs (dried)
- Gravy powder
- Couscous
- Pasta: different shapes
- Rice: brown rice, white long-grain and arborio
- Shelf-stable noodles
- Peanut butter
- Honey
- Olive oil and vegetable oil
- Cooking oil spray
- White vinegar
- Tinned tomato soup
- Tinned diced tomatoes

- Tinned corn kernels
- Tinned chickpeas (garbanzo beans)
- Tinned coconut milk
- Tinned tuna
- Sauces: Worcestershire, soy, hoisin, oyster, tomato (ketchup), barbecue (spiced ketchup)
- Powdered stock: chicken, vegetable, beef
- Curry powder
- Dried herbs and spices
- Chia seeds
- Cereals, such as Cornflakes and Weet-Bix (wheat breakfast biscuit)

FRIDGE
- Milk
- Butter or margarine
- Cheese
- Eggs
- Sour cream
- Ham
- Yoghurt
- Fresh vegetables, such as onions, mushrooms, carrots, zucchini (courgettes), potatoes, pumpkin (squash)
- Seasonal fresh fruit
- Crushed garlic in a jar
- Crushed ginger in a jar

FREEZER
- Vegetables, such as peas, corn, stir-fry mixture, spinach
- Potato chips (fries)
- Minced (ground) meat
- Sausages
- Chicken cuts (breasts, thighs, legs)

- Puff pastry sheets
- Bananas
- Berries
- Back-up muffins, cakes, etc
- Dinner leftovers

After asking the Facebook community and looking into my pantry, fridge and freezer, these were the most popular items. This list may look a little different for your family but I hope it gives you guidelines to work from.

A well-stocked pantry, fridge and freezer is your key to making mealtimes even easier.

What Should go into a healthy lunchbox?

Mandy, from Little People Nutrition, recommends a well-balanced lunchbox and shows you how easy it is to achieve this.

1. FIRSTLY, PUT IN SOMETHING YOUR CHILD WILL EAT!

There is no point making a quinoa and fig salad if your child won't eat the damn thing! Simplicity is key, ease of eating is key and, sadly, in Australia speed is key, as the kids really don't get much time to eat if they want to get up and play, especially when they get older and don't have a teacher looking over their shoulder to make sure they eat.

2. FROM A NUTRITIONALLY BALANCED POINT OF VIEW, EACH LUNCHBOX SHOULD HAVE: VEGIES OF SOME SORT, PROTEIN OF SOME SORT, CARBOHYDRATES OF SOME SORT, FRUIT OF SOME SORT, AND SOMETHING RICH IN CALCIUM

Sounds like a lot, but there is some method in this madness . . .

The reason for these recommendations is sound and extensive research by the National Health and Medical Research Council (NHMRC) based on Australian Dietary Guidelines as well as studies that have shown which food groups and macronutrients children are lacking or where they are obtaining their energy from (for example, the New South Wales Schools Physical Activity and Nutrition Survey, 2010).

Vegetables. Vegies are important because no one in Australia—kids or adults—is getting enough vegies in their diet. If a five year old is supposed to be having four serves, they are not going to eat all of that at dinner time, so let's start them on vegies early in the day.

Protein. There is no real issue with protein consumption in Australia, especially in adults, but the key for protein is to balance out the energy release of the other foods for the day and to avoid having too much quick energy and the resulting slump in mood afterwards. Protein doesn't have to be meat per se; it can be legumes, dairy, seeds or spreads of some sort.

Carbohydrates. Carbs are not just bread and pasta; they are found in fruits and even dairy, but a good wholegrain carbohydrate source for gut health and energy plays an important role in the daily energy intake of children. Mix it up with your grain sources. If you are gluten-sensitive or have coeliac disease, there are some fabulous options these days too.

Fruit. Fruit, surprisingly is also an area for concern with kids as they start to substitute their fruit intake with fruit juice. With the growing fruit juice or juicing trend, it is important to point out that one of the main reasons we eat fruit (and vegetables) is not only for their amazing vitamins and minerals, but also fibre. Fibre is incredibly important for gut and bowel health, heart health and also in assisting children to feel full. Drinking our vitamins isn't really as satisfying as eating our vitamins.

Calcium. One key area of research which does stand out is that, as children start school, their calcium intake often reduces because they are not consuming as much milk as they did as a preschooler or younger child. Of course, you can obtain calcium from other sources such as leafy green vegetables, salmon, legumes, nuts and seeds, but it takes much more of these foods to get the same calcium as from a snack of milk or cheese.

Breakfast

The most important meal of the day doesn't
have to be all cereal and toast.

BLUEBERRY BLAST SMOOTHIE

SERVES 1

Busy mornings call for quick smoothies; ones that keep you full and satisfied. This smoothie is thick and creamy and packed full of ingredients to keep your tummy happy. It does have peanut butter in it, which adds to the lovely thick texture and flavour. If you can't have nuts simply omit this ingredient.

INGREDIENTS

1 frozen banana
½ cup (70 g/2 ½ oz) frozen blueberries
a handful of baby spinach leaves
1 tablespoon peanut butter
¼ cup (25 g/1 oz) instant oats
4 ice cubes
milk, to cover the ingredients (use milk or substitute of your choice)

LET'S PUT IT ALL TOGETHER

1. Using a personal blender (I use the Kambrook Blitz2Go) or an upright blender, put all of the ingredients in together. Pulse until all ingredients are broken down and you are left with a lovely thick smoothie. Enjoy straight away.

BANANA, MANGO AND GINGER SMOOTHIE

The addition of ginger to this smoothie gives it a real kick of flavour and it is a great start to the day. The frozen fruits make this thick and creamy.

INGREDIENTS

1 frozen banana
½ frozen mango
½ cup (125 ml/4 fl oz) almond milk
½ cup (125 ml/4 fl oz) cold water
2 slivers of fresh ginger

LET'S PUT IT ALL TOGETHER

1. Put all of the ingredients in an upright blender or a personal blender (such as the Kambrook Blitz2Go) and blend until smooth. Enjoy.

MORNING MOVER BANANA SMOOTHIE

SERVES 1

This isn't just any ordinary banana smoothie, it is a complete meal that fills little tummies up with all the good things they need to get their day going. You can easily blend this up in under a minute, so it's great for when you are in a hurry and might have to drink it on the way to school or work.

INGREDIENTS

1 ripe banana (fresh or frozen)
300 ml (10½ fl oz) milk
1 Weet-Bix (wheat breakfast biscuit)
1 tablespoon honey
1 teaspoon chia seeds, 1 teaspoon ground cinnamon (optional)

LET'S PUT IT ALL TOGETHER

1. Put all of the ingredients in a blender and blend until well combined. Pour into a glass or travel cup and enjoy.

STRAWBERRY CHOCOLATE DREAM

SERVES 1

Combining two of my favourite foods into one perfect breakfast smoothie seems too good to be true. This will keep you going well into the morning.

INGREDIENTS

6 strawberries, fresh or frozen

½ banana, frozen

1 cup (250 ml/9 fl oz) milk (or substitute of your choice)

1 tablespoon unsweetened cocoa powder

½ cup (65 g/2½ oz) your favourite muesli

LET'S PUT IT ALL TOGETHER

1. Put all of the ingredients in a blender and blend until well combined. Pour into a glass or a travel cup and enjoy.

COCONUT GREEN SMOOTHIE

SERVES 1

Start your day the green way. This is a family-friendly green smoothie that is lightly sweet. If the younger family members don't enjoy green foods, try pouring the smoothie into a fun cup with a lid and straw to make them more interested.

INGREDIENTS

1 cup (250 ml/9 fl oz) drinking coconut milk

½ cup (25 g/1 oz) baby spinach

1 apple, peeled, cored and chopped

1 frozen banana

1 tablespoon honey or rice malt syrup (optional)

LET'S PUT IT ALL TOGETHER

1. Put all of the ingredients in a blender and blend until well combined. Pour into a glass or travel cup and enjoy.

OVERNIGHT CHIA SEED PUDDING

SERVES 1

Whip this up the night before and wake up to breakfast already made. The chia seeds absorb the liquid and swell up, giving you a thick pudding that will provide you with nutrients and keep you full and ready to tackle the day.

INGREDIENTS

3 tablespoons chia seeds
3 tablespoons Greek yoghurt
100 ml (3½ fl oz) milk
½ teaspoon natural vanilla essence
1 tablespoon honey
a handful of frozen mixed berries (optional)
Topping: fresh sliced banana, seeds like sunflower or pepitas, sultanas (golden raisins)

LET'S PUT IT ALL TOGETHER

1. In a glass jar or container with a tight-fitting lid, combine all of the ingredients (except the toppings). Put the lid on and give it a good shake. Stand in the fridge. Before you go to bed, give it another good shake or stir with a spoon, as you will find some clumping of the chia seeds at the bottom.
2. In the morning the chia seeds will be completely swelled up and you will have a pudding consistency. Top with sliced banana and the seed and sultana mix.

OVERNIGHT OATS IN A JAR (OIAJ)

OIAJ is a little like Bircher muesli, except that you can make it in a jar so that it is convenient to take with you when you are a hurry. It's super-easy to put together.

INGREDIENTS

½ cup (50 g/1¾ oz) rolled (porridge) oats or muesli
½ cup (125 ml/4 fl oz) milk (or substitute of your choice)
3 tablespoons Greek yoghurt
1 teaspoon honey
½ cup (100 g/3½ oz) grated apple

LET'S PUT IT ALL TOGETHER

1. Put all of the ingredients into a jar with a tight-fitting lid and shake, shake, shake. Stand in the fridge overnight.
2. In the morning you will have a thick and creamy breakfast ready to be eaten as is or with extra fruits and nuts added.
3. In colder weather you can even heat it in the microwave to warm it through. Simply leave in the glass jar or place in a microwave-safe bowl and heat on high for 30 seconds.

THREE-INGREDIENT BANANA PANCAKES

MAKES 12 SMALL PANCAKES

Three ingredients is all you need to make these simply delicious pancakes. Eat them for breakfast, send them to school in a lunchbox or enjoy them for morning tea topped with chocolate spread and strawberries or peanut butter and banana slices. However you serve them you will be making these again and again.

INGREDIENTS

2 large bananas: you want to use ones that are perfectly ripe, not overripe

3 extra-large eggs

½ cup (70 g/2½ oz) self-raising flour (you can use gluten-free flour if you need to)

butter, for frying

LET'S PUT IT ALL TOGETHER

1. Using a food processor, blender, personal blender or Thermomix, process the bananas, eggs and flour together until a smooth batter is formed, in about 10–20 seconds.

2. Heat a non-stick frying pan over medium–high heat. Rub a little butter on the heated pan and pour in the pancake batter to make the desired-size pancakes. Cook for 1 minute, then flip and cook for 1 minute on the other side. Repeat until all the batter is used.

EASY TRADITIONAL PANCAKES

Traditional pancakes are a favourite weekend food.
Because they are made from basic ingredients, you
can quickly and easily create something amazing for
breakfast. I like to top mine with strawberries and peanut
butter, while lemon and sugar is my husband's choice and
the boys love butter and sprinkles.
These are also freezer-friendly and perfect
for lunchboxes.

INGREDIENTS

2 cups (300 g/10½ oz) self-raising flour
¼ teaspoon bicarbonate of soda (baking soda)
⅓ cup (75 g/2¾ oz) caster (superfine) sugar
1¾ cups (435 ml/15¼ fl oz) milk
1 teaspoon white vinegar
2 eggs
1 teaspoon natural vanilla essence
butter or cooking spray, for frying

LET'S PUT IT ALL TOGETHER

1. Put all of the ingredients into a large mixing bowl and whisk
   together until well combined. Set aside to stand for 5 minutes or
   until little bubbles form on the surface.

2. Heat a little butter or cooking spray in a frying pan over medium heat. Pour the pancake batter into the pan until the pancake is the desired size. Cook on one side until bubbles appear on the surface, then flip and cook for a further minute. Repeat until all of the batter is used.

APPLE AND CINNAMON PANCAKES

MAKES 12+

This is a classic combination of apple and cinnamon
in a pancake. No need to top these pancakes with
anything extra, because all the flavour is already in them.
They are also a great way to increase your
family's fruit intake.

INGREDIENTS

1 cup (150 g/5½ oz) self-raising flour
1 tablespoon sugar
1 egg
1 cup (250 ml/9 fl oz) milk
1 apple, grated
1 teaspoon ground cinnamon
butter or cooking spray, for frying

LET'S PUT IT ALL TOGETHER

1. Put the flour, sugar, egg and milk into a bowl and stir with a whisk
   to combine. It should be a runny but firm texture. Add the apple
   and cinnamon and combine. Set aside to stand for 5–10 minutes
   until bubbles form on the surface.

2. Heat a little butter or cooking spray in a frying pan over medium heat. Pour the pancake batter into the pan until the pancake is the desired size. Cook on one side until bubbles appear on the surface, then flip and cook for a further minute. Repeat until all of the batter is used.

PANCAKE BITES

These pancake bites use a simple pancake batter,
which is poured into a mini muffin tin, topped with
your favourite toppings and then baked.
Voila! Twenty-four delicious pancake bites
ready to enjoy for Sunday breakfast or to pack
in a lunchbox.

INGREDIENTS

1 cup (150 g/5½ oz) self-raising flour
¼ teaspoon bicarbonate of soda (baking soda)
1 egg
1½ cups (375 ml/13 fl oz) milk
butter or cooking spray, for greasing
Toppings, such as blueberries, bananas, strawberry jam, Nutella,
    peanut butter
Greek yoghurt, to serve

LET'S PUT IT ALL TOGETHER

1. Preheat the oven to 180°C (350°F). Grease the holes of a
   24-hole mini muffin tin.
2. In a medium bowl, whisk together all of the ingredients except
   the toppings and yoghurt. Whisk until well combined.
3. Pour the batter evenly into the holes of the 24-hole mini muffin
   tin, then place the chosen toppings in the batter.

4. Bake for 15 minutes or until lightly golden.
5. Allow to cool before removing the pancake bites from the tin. Serve with the yoghurt and extra fruit or enjoy on their own.

BANANA BREAKFAST BISCUITS

MAKES 24

Breakfast in a biscuit (cookie)! Perfect for fussy eaters (who love biscuits), these are a well-balanced alternative to a traditional breakfast.

INGREDIENTS

2 ripe bananas, mashed
2 eggs
½ cup (175 g/6 oz) honey
½ cup (125 ml/4 fl oz) sunflower oil
1½ cups (220 g/7¾ oz) wholemeal (whole wheat) self-raising flour
1 cup (95 g/3¼ oz) rolled (porridge) oats
4 tablespoons peanut butter (or hulled tahini)
chocolate chips, to sprinkle on top (optional)

LET'S PUT IT ALL TOGETHER

1. Preheat the oven to 180°C (350°F). Line a baking tray with baking paper and set aside.
2. Put all of the ingredients into a bowl and mix well to combine. The biscuit mix will be slightly runnier than a normal biscuit mix.
3. Drop tablespoon amounts onto the prepared baking tray. Leave 2 cm between each biscuit.
4. Bake for 12–15 minutes until lightly golden.
5. Transfer to a wire rack to cool completely.

BLUEBERRY AND YOGHURT BREAKFAST MUFFINS

MAKES 12

Keep some of these in the freezer and you will always have something for breakfast. Enjoy with a smoothie and everyone is ready to start the day.

INGREDIENTS

¾ cup (110 g/3¾ oz) self-raising flour
¼ cup (35 g/1¼ oz) wholemeal (whole wheat) self-raising flour
¼ cup (55 g/2 oz) raw (unrefined) sugar
1 cup (95 g/3¼ oz) rolled (porridge) oats
1 cup (260 g/9¼ oz) vanilla-flavoured yoghurt
1 egg
1 cup (125 g/4½ oz) frozen blueberries

LET'S PUT IT ALL TOGETHER

1. Preheat the oven to 180°C (350°F). Line the holes of a 12-hole standard muffin tin with paper cases and set aside.
2. Put all of the ingredients (except the blueberries) into a large mixing bowl and stir to just combine. Stir through the blueberries.
3. Pour into the prepared muffin tin and bake for 15–20 minutes until lightly golden. They should bounce back when touched. Remove from the oven and allow to cool in the tin.

ONE-MINUTE BREAKFAST PARFAIT

This is such an easy breakfast option that it can be put together in less than a minute. And who doesn't love a breakfast that looks like a dessert?

INGREDIENTS

1 cup (125 g/4½ oz) toasted muesli (use your favourite combination)
4 tablespoons plain yoghurt
strawberries or banana slices, to serve

LET'S PUT IT ALL TOGETHER

1. In a glass or a parfait glass, spoon in a layer of toasted muesli followed by a tablespoon of yoghurt and repeat until all the ingredients are used. Top with fresh strawberries or banana slices.

FRENCH RAISIN TOAST

MAKES 4 SERVES

I love raisin toast on its own, but when you make it into French toast it becomes the perfect Sunday breakfast. Serve with fresh fruits, a dollop of yoghurt and a drizzle of maple syrup. It looks impressive without a lot of effort.

INGREDIENTS

2 eggs
½ cup (125 ml/4 fl oz) milk
4 slices of raisin bread (thick slices work the best)
butter, for frying

LET'S PUT IT ALL TOGETHER

1. In a large bowl, combine the eggs and milk and whisk together. Dip one slice of raisin bread into the egg mixture, making sure both sides of the bread are well coated.
2. Melt a tablespoon of butter in a frying pan over medium heat and add the soaked raisin bread. Cook for 1 minute, then flip and cook for a further minute. Repeat with the remaining slices of raisin bread.

BAKED MINI OMELETTES

MAKES 12

Omelettes can sometimes be time consuming when everyone wants a different filling. These baked mini omelettes solve that problem. You can easily keep everyone happy by making 12 different mini omelettes at once.

INGREDIENTS

8 eggs
½ cup (125 ml/4 fl oz) thin (pouring) cream
cooking spray, for greasing
1 cup chopped vegetables, such as mushrooms, tomato, baby spinach, capsicum, etc
1 cup diced meats, such as ham, bacon, sausage, salami
1 cup (100 g/3½ oz) grated tasty cheddar cheese

LET'S PUT IT ALL TOGETHER

1. Preheat the oven to 200°C (400°F).
2. Crack the eggs into a large mixing bowl, add the cream, season with salt and pepper and whisk to combine.
3. Spray a 12-hole standard muffin tin with cooking spray. Put the chopped vegetables and meat into each hole (filling each hole to halfway). Pour in the egg mixture to cover the chopped ingredients. Top with a sprinkling of grated cheese.

4. Bake for 15 minutes or until the omelettes puff up and are lightly golden. (Note: they will flatten when cooled.)
5. Enjoy straight away or store in an airtight container in the fridge and reheat in the microwave.

MICROWAVE SCRAMBLED EGGS

SERVES 1

In a hurry, but still want to enjoy a hot breakfast before you start your day? These herby microwaved eggs are just what you need. In the time it takes to cook a piece of toast you will have scrambled eggs as well.

INGREDIENTS

1 egg
a dash of milk
a sprinkling of your favourite dried herb, like basil or parsley
bread, for toasting

LET'S PUT IT ALL TOGETHER

1. Crack the egg into a coffee mug, then add the milk and herbs, and season with salt and pepper. Use a fork to give it a good whisk.
2. Place the mug in the microwave and set it on high for 1 minute and 30 seconds. You may need to add or subtract from the time depending on the wattage of your microwave.
3. While the egg is cooking, pop a slice of bread into the toaster. They should both be ready at nearly the same time.
4. Give the egg a bit of a stir in the mug, then spoon it onto the toast.

CHEESY CORN FRITTERS

MAKES ABOUT 12

I always have a packet of frozen corn kernels in the freezer so I can whip these up when we are after a substantial meal that is still quick and easy. Tinned corn kernels also work just as well.

INGREDIENTS

2 cups (300 g/10½ oz) frozen corn kernels, thawed
½ cup (50 g/1¾ oz) grated tasty cheddar cheese
½ cup (70 g/2½ oz) plain (all-purpose) flour
½ teaspoon pepper
½ teaspoon salt
2 eggs, whisked
⅓ cup (80 ml/2½ fl oz) olive oil

LET'S PUT IT ALL TOGETHER

1. In a large bowl combine the corn, cheese, flour, pepper and salt. Mix well to coat the cheese and corn in the flour. Add the whisked egg and stir well to combine.
2. Heat a large non-stick frying pan over medium heat and put in the olive oil. Once the oil is heated, add tablespoon amounts of the batter, leaving enough room to flip them over. Cook for 3 minutes on one side and then flip and cook for a further 2 minutes. Both sides should be golden in colour. Repeat with the remaining batter.

BREAKFAST PUFF SQUARES

MAKES 4

....

Having puff pastry in the freezer is such a time saver.
It gives you the versatility to make quick meals without fuss.
You can make as many of these breakfast puffs as your
oven will take, so they are perfect for feeding a crowd.

....

INGREDIENTS

4 sheets of frozen puff pastry, thawed

8 eggs

4 tomato slices

4 rindless bacon rashers (or slices of ham)

1 cup (100 g/3½ oz) grated tasty cheddar cheese

LET'S PUT IT ALL TOGETHER

1. Preheat the oven to 200°C (400°F). Line a baking tray with baking paper and lay a puff pastry sheet on it. Fold each edge of the pastry over by about 2 cm (¾ inch) to form a raised border.
2. Crack 2 eggs into the pastry case. Add a slice of tomato and a rasher of bacon, season with salt and pepper and scatter with one-quarter of the cheese. Repeat with the remaining ingredients.
3. Bake for 10 minutes or until the pastry is puffed up and golden.
4. Best enjoyed straight from the oven.

THE BEST TOAST TOPPINGS

Toast is the most requested breakfast food in our house, so I am always looking for different topping combinations to keep things interesting and tasty. Here is a list of toppings that everyone enjoys.

- Peanut butter, sliced banana and honey
- Peanut butter, apple slices and ground cinnamon
- Cottage cheese, sliced banana and honey
- Ricotta, sliced pears and honey
- Cream cheese and blueberries
- Mashed avocado, lemon juice, salt and pepper
- Ham, tomato and melted cheese
- Avocado and melted cheese
- Avocado and a fried egg
- Cream cheese and smoked salmon
- Vegemite and melted cheese
- Garlic mushrooms
- Strawberry jam and ricotta
- Bacon, banana and melted cheese

What's your favourite combination? Share them with me on my blog, Facebook or Instagram page using the hashtag #cookingforbusymumscookbook

SOUPS

Have your family eating all the colours of the rainbow with these tasty and nutritious soups.

These recipes all take 30 minutes or less to make and most of this is cooking time, so you are free to do other things while your pot bubbles away on the stove.

A little tip to make soups family friendly so the youngest members of the family enjoy them:

I pour the soup over cooked pasta and they go crazy for it.

Also, dippy soldiers (toast fingers) does the trick to make them eat soups happily in our house. What's your trick?

SWEET POTATO SOUP

SERVES 4–6

This recipe for sweet potato soup is easy-peasy and has a lovely naturally sweet flavour, making it popular with the little ones in the house.
Grab a pot and some vegetables and you'll be enjoying this soup in 30 minutes.

INGREDIENTS

1 tablespoon olive oil

1 onion, sliced

1 tablespoon crushed garlic

2 sweet potatoes, peeled and cut into even chunks (the smaller the chunks, the quicker it will cook)

2 potatoes, peeled and cut into even chunks

2 zucchini (courgettes), peeled and cut into chunks

8 cups (2 litres/70 fl oz) vegetable stock (enough to cover the vegetables)

cream and finely chopped fresh parsley, to serve (optional)

LET'S PUT IT ALL TOGETHER

1. Put the olive oil, onion and garlic into a large saucepan over medium–high heat for 1 minute.

2. Add the remaining vegetables and pour in the vegetable stock to cover the vegetables. Season with salt and pepper. Bring to the boil, then cover with a lid and reduce to a simmer for 30 minutes or until all the vegetables are soft when pierced with a knife. Remove from the heat and allow to cool slightly.

3. Using a stick blender, process the vegetables to make a smooth soup.
4. Serve with a drizzle of cream and scattered with fresh parsley, if you like. My boys like this with toast dippers.

CARROT AND COCONUT SOUP

SERVES 4–6

These three ingredients, when combined, create the most perfect winter soup that is budget-friendly, tasty and, most importantly, good for you.

INGREDIENTS

1 tablespoon olive oil
1 kg (2 lb 4 oz) carrots, cut into 2 cm (¾ inch) chunks
1 onion, sliced
400 ml (14 fl oz) light coconut cream
1 teaspoon ground turmeric
400 ml (14 fl oz) vegetable stock

LET'S PUT IT ALL TOGETHER

1. Put the olive oil, carrot and onion into a large saucepan over high heat and cook for a minute or two.
2. Add the remaining ingredients, bring to the boil and then reduce to a simmer, cooking with the lid on for 20 minutes or until the carrot is tender.
3. Using a stick blender, blitz until smooth. If it is too thick, add a little water.

BROCCOLI AND BACON SOUP

SERVES 4–6

This has to be my favourite soup to make. It tastes delicious, has a bright green colour and will easily satisfy a hungry stomach.

INGREDIENTS

olive oil, for frying

1 onion, chopped

4 garlic cloves, thinly sliced

4 bacon rashers, rind removed, chopped

2 large heads of broccoli, cut into segments

2 potatoes, peeled and quartered

8 cups (2 litres/70 fl oz) chicken stock (or enough to just cover all the ingredients)

⅔ cup (100 g/3½ oz) frozen peas

½ cup (125 ml/4 fl oz) thickened (whipping) cream

crusty bread, cream, grated parmesan cheese, to serve (optional)

LET'S PUT IT ALL TOGETHER

1. In a large saucepan over high heat, put the olive oil, onion, garlic and bacon. Cook, stirring regularly, until the onion and garlic start to soften.
2. Add the broccoli and potato followed by enough chicken stock to cover everything.
3. Simmer over medium–low heat for 30–45 minutes until the broccoli and potato soften.

4. Remove from the heat and add the peas (this will brighten the soup colour) and cream and season with pepper.
5. Using a stick blender, blitz until relatively smooth.
6. Enjoy with crusty bread and a dollop of cream and a sprinkle of parmesan cheese if you like.

CAULIFLOWER SOUP

SERVES 4–6

Cauliflower soup is one of the most versatile soups: the addition of some grated cheese turns it into a healthy white sauce to use in pasta bakes, lasagne and more. It also tastes better than it smells.

INGREDIENTS
1 onion, sliced
4 garlic cloves, thinly sliced
olive oil, for frying
1 head of cauliflower, cut into small chunks
4 potatoes, peeled and cut into small chunks
8 cups (2 litres/70 fl oz) chicken or vegetable stock
½ cup (125 ml/4 fl oz) skim (no-fat) milk
a sprinkle of pepper (I use black pepper, but you can use white
    pepper if you don't want to see it)

LET'S PUT IT ALL TOGETHER
1. In a large saucepan over medium heat, put the onion, garlic and a splash of olive oil. Cook them until the onion softens.
2. Add the cauliflower, potato and enough stock to just cover the vegetables. Simmer on medium heat for 25 minutes or until all the vegetables are soft.
3. Remove from the heat and add the milk and salt and pepper to taste. Use a stick blender to blitz to a smooth creamy consistency.

QUICK PUMPKIN SOUP

SERVES 4–6

Grab your grater (or food processor) for this quick pumpkin soup. It takes no time to cook, which is handy for busy nights. For a tasty variation, add 1 tablespoon of curry powder or paste.

INGREDIENTS

1 tablespoon olive oil

1 onion, chopped

2 garlic cloves, sliced

1 butternut pumpkin (squash), peeled, deseeded and flesh grated

4 potatoes, peeled and grated

4 cups (1 litre/35 fl oz) chicken or vegetable stock

½ cup (125 g/4½ oz) sour cream

croutons, to serve (optional)

LET'S PUT IT ALL TOGETHER

1. Heat a large saucepan over medium–high heat and add the olive oil, onion and garlic. Cook, stirring, for 1 minute. Add the grated pumpkin and potato and cook, stirring, for an additional minute.
2. Add the stock to cover all the vegetables and simmer for 10 minutes, making sure to stir during this time. Once the vegetables are soft, remove the soup from the heat.
3. Add the sour cream and use a stick blender to blend until smooth.
4. Enjoy with croutons for a crunchy hit.

CHEAT'S CHICKEN AND CORN NOODLE SOUP

SERVES 4–6

Turn your leftover roast chicken into this quick and easy chicken and corn noodle soup. There's nothing like getting a second meal from leftovers.

INGREDIENTS

8 cups (2 litres/70 fl oz) chicken stock
1 cup (90 g/3¼ oz) dry noodles, such as angel hair pasta or vermicelli
about ½ roasted chicken, meat picked
400 g (14 oz) tin creamed corn
1 spring onion (scallion), thinly sliced

LET'S PUT IT ALL TOGETHER

1. In a large saucepan over medium–high heat, bring the chicken stock to the boil.
2. Add the dry noodles and simmer for 15 minutes.
3. Add the chicken meat, creamed corn and spring onion. Season with pepper, stir and allow to heat through for another 5 minutes.
4. Once the noodles are soft to bite the soup is ready.

TIP As you are using leftover roasted meat, this should be eaten the day it is made.

QUICK PEA AND HAM SOUP

SERVES 4–6

The traditional pea and ham soup can take hours to cook, but this one throws tradition out the door and still gives you the same great-tasting filling soup you love.

INGREDIENTS

olive oil, for frying
1 onion, chopped
1 garlic clove, thinly sliced
1 carrot, thinly sliced
2 celery stalks, thinly sliced
3⅓ cups (500 g/1 lb 2 oz) frozen peas
2 potatoes, peeled and finely chopped
4 cups (1 litre/35 fl oz) chicken stock
300 g (10½ oz) ham, diced

LET'S PUT IT ALL TOGETHER

1. In a large saucepan over medium–high heat, put the olive oil, onion and garlic and cook for 1 minute to soften. Add the carrot and celery and cook for a further minute.
2. Reduce to medium heat, add the peas and potato and cook for 5 minutes, stirring regularly.

3. Add the chicken stock and 1 cup (250 ml/9 fl oz) of water and reduce to a simmer for 15 minutes or until the potato is cooked through. Remove from the heat and use a stick blender to blend until smooth.

4. Return the soup to the stove over low heat and add the diced ham. Cook for a further 5 minutes before serving.

TOMATO AND BACON SOUP

SERVES 4–6

Tomato and bacon are a match made in heaven. Full of big flavours, this makes a great starter to your meal.

INGREDIENTS

2 tablespoons olive oil

1 onion, chopped

1 garlic clove, thinly sliced

6 bacon rashers, rind removed, chopped

1 leek, finely sliced

2 celery stalks, chopped

2 × 400 g (14 oz) tins whole tomatoes

6 cups (1.5 litres/52 fl oz) chicken stock

1 potato, peeled and diced

1 teaspoon dried basil

2 teaspoons sugar

2 dry bay leaves

croutons, to serve (optional)

LET'S PUT IT ALL TOGETHER

1. In a large saucepan over medium–high heat, add the olive oil, onion, garlic and bacon. Cook for 2 minutes or until the vegetables start to soften.

2. Add the leek and celery and cook for a further 3 minutes or until the leek has softened. Add the tomatoes, stock, potato, basil, sugar and bay leaves and stir well. Cover with a lid and simmer over low heat for 15 minutes.
3. Before blending, remove the bay leaves. Use a stick blender to blend gently: you don't want it to be too smooth. Season with salt and pepper to taste and some croutons to serve, if you like.

Light Meals and Side Dishes

Lunch normally consists of leftovers during the week, but when we are home on the weekends I love nothing more than to cook lunch, sit outside in the sunshine and enjoy it with my family. These meals are quick and easy and make enough to enjoy for another meal.

MICROWAVE POTATO SALAD

Potato salad is a barbecue staple and it is also delicious with a slice of ham in a fresh bread roll. I use the microwave and baby potatoes to speed this recipe up; of course, if you don't have a microwave you can boil the potatoes on the stovetop.

INGREDIENTS

1.5 kg (3 lb 5 oz) baby potatoes

3 eggs

1 small red onion

2 spring onions (scallions)

¾ cup (185 g/6½ oz) whole egg mayonnaise

½ cup (125 g/4½ oz) sour cream

3 tablespoons dijon mustard

LET'S PUT IT ALL TOGETHER

1. Wash the baby potatoes and put them on a microwave-safe plate. Cook in the microwave for 8 minutes on high. If a knife goes through the potato easily, they are cooked. If not, cook for a further 2 minutes. (Time will vary depending on the microwave.)
2. While the potatoes are cooking, hard-boil the eggs, chop the red onion and spring onions and make the dressing.

3. To make the dressing, mix the mayonnaise, sour cream, mustard and a sprinkling of salt and pepper.
4. Once the potatoes are cooked, cut them into quarters and put them in the fridge to cool. Peel the eggs and cut them into quarters as well, then add them to the potatoes in the fridge.
5. When the potatoes are coolish, add the red onion and spring onions and stir through the dressing.

BLT PASTA SALAD

Pasta isn't only reserved for hot dishes, it is great as a salad too. I love a good BLT and this salad has all the flavour of the popular sandwich combined with pasta to create a fantastic side dish. It is also a great dish to take to a barbecue.

INGREDIENTS

200 g (7 oz) rindless streaky bacon rashes, sliced

¼ cup (60 g/2¼ oz) whole egg mayonnaise

¼ cup (65 g/2½ oz) sour cream

3 tablespoons wholegrain mustard

4 cups (700 g/1 lb 9 oz) cooked spiral pasta, cooled

250 g (9 oz) cherry tomatoes, halved

2 cups (80 g/2¾ oz) shredded iceberg lettuce

LET'S PUT IT ALL TOGETHER

1. Heat a frying pan over high heat and cook the bacon until crunchy.
2. Prepare the dressing by mixing together the mayonnaise, sour cream and mustard, then season with salt and pepper.
3. In a large bowl, put the cooled pasta, tomatoes and lettuce and mix gently to combine. Drizzle the dressing over and toss through. Top with the crunchy bacon just before serving.

 TIP Cook the pasta the night before or early in the morning and have it cooled ready to assemble the salad.

FRESH BROCCOLI AND APPLE SALAD WITH AVOCADO DRESSING

SERVES 6–8 AS A SIDE OR 4 AS A MAIN

I love fresh broccoli (I always eat the stalks when
I cut it up for our roast dinner) and this salad makes
the most of them. The apples and sultanas add a lovely
sweet twist and the avocado dressing gives it a creamy
tang to bring it all together. This is a nutritious
work lunch or side dish.

INGREDIENTS

1 head of broccoli, cut into small florets
2 red apples, cored and thinly sliced
1 carrot, grated
1 small onion, thinly sliced
⅓ cup (60 g/2¼ oz) sultanas (golden raisins)

Avocado Dressing

1 avocado
juice of ½ lemon
½ cup (125 ml/4 fl oz) thin (pouring) cream

LET'S PUT IT ALL TOGETHER

1. Combine the broccoli, apple, carrot and onion in a large
    serving bowl.

2. In a separate small bowl, make the avocado dressing: mash the avocado flesh and add the lemon and cream. Season with salt and pepper to taste. Mix well.

3. Pour the dressing over the ingredients in the large bowl, add the sultanas and mix to ensure everything gets a good coating.

BROWN RICE SALAD

SERVES 4–6

I love brown rice: it has a hearty flavour and is packed full of fibre. This is a satisfying combination of sweet, salty and crunchy. You can enjoy this dish hot or cold; it really is a throw-it-all-together meal that you can prepare in no time.

INGREDIENTS

4 cups (740 g/1 lb 10 oz) cooked brown rice

2 carrots, grated

½ cup (85 g/3 oz) sultanas (golden raisins)

4 tablespoons crushed peanuts

4 tablespoons soy sauce (low sodium)

chopped fresh parsley or alfalfa sprouts, to serve (optional)

LET'S PUT IT ALL TOGETHER

1. Simply combine all of the ingredients in a medium bowl and mix gently.

ZUCCHINI AND BACON SLICE

MAKES 16 SLICES

We love this zucchini and bacon slice in our family and I like it even more because my fussy little green-avoiding eaters will actually eat it. Keep it in the fridge so that you can grab a slice whenever you like (it never lasts longer than three days in our house), pack a slice in the work or school lunchbox, eat it as an easy and nutritious breakfast on the run, or enjoy it warm for dinner. It really is a versatile little slice.

INGREDIENTS

3 zucchini (courgettes)
2 carrots
1 onion
200 g (7 oz) rindless streaky bacon rashers (I use D'Orsogna), chopped
½ cup (75 g/2¾ oz) plain (all-purpose) flour
1 cup (100 g/3½ oz) grated cheddar cheese
5 eggs

LET'S PUT IT ALL TOGETHER

1. Preheat the oven to 160°C (315°F). Line a 20-cm (8-inch) square baking dish with baking paper and set aside.
2. I find that using a food processor to prepare the ingredients makes it a lot quicker and easier. Grate the vegetables first and squeeze out all excess liquid. This is important to make sure your slice doesn't turn out messy. Once you have squeezed out the liquid, put the grated vegetables into a large bowl.

3. Add the bacon, flour and cheese, then season with salt and pepper to taste. Mix well to coat all the ingredients.

4. Whisk the eggs in a jug and pour them into the bowl. Mix well to combine. Pour the mixture into the prepared baking dish and bake for 50 minutes or until the slice is golden and mostly firm to touch.

5. Enjoy warm or allow to cool.

HAM AND ZUCCHINI FRITTATA

SERVES 4

Frittata is a simple dish to make when you are running low on ingredients. You can stretch what you've got to get you through. Eggs are the main ingredient of a frittata and it is crustless which means it's really easy to put together and is gluten free.

INGREDIENTS

3 zucchini (courgettes), grated
4 ham slices, cut into fine strips
1 cup (100 g/3½ oz) grated cheddar cheese
1 small onion, chopped
2 tablespoons chives, finely chopped
4 eggs
1 cup (250 g/9 oz) coconut cream, or use thin (pouring) cream

LET'S PUT IT ALL TOGETHER

1. Preheat the oven to 180°C (350°F). Grease a 25-cm (10-inch) pie dish and set aside.
2. Put all of the ingredients into a large bowl and mix to combine. Season with salt and pepper.
3. Pour into the prepared pie dish and bake for 45 minutes or until set.
4. Serve with a side salad and some oven-baked chips to make a complete meal. Also great served cold the next day for lunch.

LEFTOVER ROAST VEGETABLE FRITTATA LOAF

SERVES 4–6

Don't throw out leftover roast vegetables
(you might even want to cook extra vegies
so you can make this dish): they make a
delicious filling for a light and fluffy frittata.

INGREDIENTS

6 eggs

½ cup (125 g/4½ oz) sour cream

2 cups leftover roast vegetables (pumpkin, carrot, potato and
   sweet potato work well)

2 handfuls of baby spinach leaves

½ onion, finely sliced

100 g (3½ oz) feta cheese

LET'S PUT IT ALL TOGETHER

1. Preheat the oven to 190°C (375°F). Line a 20-cm (8-inch) loaf
   tin with baking paper.
2. In a medium bowl, whisk the eggs and sour cream, then season
   with salt and pepper. Stir through the remaining ingredients and
   pour into the prepared tin.
3. Bake the frittata for about 50 minutes or until it is firm to touch.

TIP As you are using leftover vegetables this is best enjoyed
1–2 days after making.

CHICKEN AND MUSHROOM QUICHE

SERVES 4–6

I sometimes buy a roast chicken just so I can make this quiche. Chicken and mushroom are a match made in heaven. This will quickly become a family favourite.

INGREDIENTS

olive oil or cooking spray, for greasing

2 sheets of frozen shortcrust (pie) pastry, thawed

4 eggs

½ cup (125 ml/4 fl oz) milk

½ cup (125 ml/4 fl oz) thin (pouring) cream

1 cup (100 g/3½ oz) grated cheddar cheese

2 cups (350 g/12 oz) shredded cooked chicken

1 cup (90 g/3¼ oz) chopped mushrooms

1 onion, chopped

side salad and oven-baked chips, to serve

LET'S PUT IT ALL TOGETHER

1. Preheat the oven to 190°C (375°F). Grease a 25-cm (10-inch) pie dish with a little olive oil or cooking spray. Line the base and side of the dish with the shortcrust pastry.

2. In a medium bowl, whisk together the eggs, milk, cream and cheese, then season with salt and pepper.
3. Add the chicken, mushrooms and onion and stir to combine. Pour into the prepared pastry case.
4. Bake for 45–55 minutes until set. Remove from the oven and stand for 5 minutes before slicing and serving with a side salad and oven-baked chips.

CHICKEN AND VEGETABLE SAUSAGE ROLLS

MAKES APPROXIMATELY 24–30
BITE-SIZE SAUSAGE ROLLS

....

These sausage rolls are not only a convenient little
parcel of food, they are also full of the good stuff,
so you don't mind the family enjoying them as a
main meal. I have used the food processor
to make this quick and easy, but you can
use a grater and your hands.

....

INGREDIENTS

1 carrot, roughly chopped
1 zucchini (courgette), roughly chopped
½ small red capsicum (pepper), roughly chopped
1 onion, roughly chopped
500 g (1 lb 2 oz) minced (ground) chicken
1 teaspoon herbs, such as thyme and oregano
2 tablespoons wholegrain mustard
2–3 sheets of frozen puff pastry, thawed
cooking oil spray or 1 egg, whisked, for brushing
sesame seeds, for sprinkling (optional)

LET'S PUT IT ALL TOGETHER

1. Preheat the oven to 200°C (400°F). Line a baking tray with baking paper and set aside.
2. In a food processor fitted with the metal chopping blade, put the roughly chopped pieces of the carrot, zucchini, capsicum and onion. Process until finely chopped. Alternatively, you can grate

the vegetables. Squeeze out the excess liquid that will come out of the vegetables once they are processed or grated.

3. Add the chicken, herbs and mustard to the food processor bowl, season with salt and pepper and process for 1 minute or until all the ingredients come together. Alternatively, you can use your hands to mix all the ingredients together well. Working the chicken mince really well is important as the mixing process works the proteins to make sure the mix holds together when cooked.

4. Take one thawed sheet of puff pasty and cut it in half. Put one-third of the chicken and vegetable mixture in a line down the centre of each half, lengthways. Roll the pastry over to form the sausage roll.

5. Repeat with the remaining pastry and chicken mixture. Cut into bite-size sausage rolls and put them onto the prepared baking tray. Spray with cooking oil or brush with the whisked egg and sprinkle with sesame seeds, if using. Bake for 15–20 minutes until lightly golden.

6. To make ahead and keep in the freezer, follow steps 2–5. Instead of cooking, freeze the sausage rolls on the baking tray and, when frozen, transfer to resealable plastic bags. When you are ready to eat them, put the frozen rolls onto a baking paper-lined baking tray and continue with step 5. They may need an extra 5 minutes of cooking time. You can store the uncooked rolls in the freezer for up to 3 months.

SAUSAGE ROLLS THE KIDS WILL LOVE

MAKES 24–32

....

These mini rolls are a satisfying vegie smuggler; they are made with real meat and the flavour is no comparison to the frozen ready-made variety.

....

INGREDIENTS

500 g (1 lb 2 oz) minced (ground) veal or beef
1 carrot, grated
1 small zucchini (courgette), peeled and grated
1 teaspoon crushed garlic
¼ onion, finely chopped
1 teaspoon wholegrain mustard
1 egg
1 teaspoon chicken stock powder, or just season with salt and
    pepper
2 sheets of frozen puff pastry, thawed
cooking oil spray

LET'S PUT IT ALL TOGETHER

1. Preheat the oven to 200°C (400°F). Line a baking tray with baking paper and set aside. Combine all of the ingredients except the puff pastry and cooking oil in a large bowl and mix well with your hands.
2. Cut a sheet of puff pastry in half, lay a quarter of the mixture along the middle of the strip of puff pastry, making sure to go all the way to the ends.

3. Roll the pastry over the mixture and all the way over to seal.
4. Cut into bite-size pieces, about 6–8 per roll. Put them on the prepared baking tray and spray with a little cooking oil.
5. Repeat with the remaining mixture and pastry.
6. Bake for 10–15 minutes until puffed up and golden brown.

CRUNCHY PARMESAN FISH FINGERS

SERVES 4

Sometimes it's difficult to get the little members of the family to eat fish. This recipe makes it fun and tasty.

INGREDIENTS

2 cups (120 g/4¼ oz) panko breadcrumbs
½ cup (50 g/1¾ oz) finely grated parmesan cheese
1 cup (150 g/5½ oz) plain (all-purpose) flour
¼ cup (60 ml/2 fl oz) milk
1 egg
500 g (1 lb 2 oz) hoki or any firm white-fleshed fish, sliced into finger-size pieces
olive oil, for frying

LET'S PUT IT ALL TOGETHER

1. Mix together the breadcrumbs and parmesan cheese. You will need two plates and a bowl to crumb the fish. Put the flour on one plate, the breadcrumb mix on the other and in a shallow bowl whisk together the milk and egg.
2. Crumb the fish fingers by first coating in the flour, then dipping them in the egg mixture and finally rolling in the breadcrumb mix.

3. In a large frying pan over medium heat, heat a shallow layer of olive oil. The oil is hot enough when a cube of bread turns golden brown in 20 seconds. Place the crumbed fish fingers gently into the oil. Cook for about 1 minute or until golden before flipping and cooking on the other side until golden. Transfer to paper towel to soak up any excess oil. Repeat until all the fish fingers have been cooked.
4. Serve with some chunky oven-baked chips, lemon wedges and tartare sauce.

TIP Best enjoyed on the day of making.

FISH AND NOODLE CAKES

MAKES 10

Grab your trusty food processor and let's get started.
The addition of noodles to these fishcakes makes
this a satisfying variant.

INGREDIENTS

125 g (4½ oz) rice vermicelli noodles
500 g (1 lb 2 oz) firm white boneless fish fillets, such as basa or
    snapper
3 tablespoons tamari oyster sauce
3 tablespoons sweet chilli sauce, plus extra, for dipping
1 tablespoon fish sauce
¼ cup (35 g/1¼ oz) plain (all-purpose) flour
2 spring onions (scallions), chopped
½ cup (15 g/½ oz) coriander (cilantro) leaves
juice of ½ lime
sunflower oil, for frying

LET'S PUT IT ALL TOGETHER

1. Put the noodles in a large bowl and cover with boiling water.
    Allow to soak for about 5 minutes until they soften. Prepare the
    other ingredients while you are waiting.
2. In a food processor fitted with the metal chopping blade,
    put the fish, tamari or oyster sauce, sweet chilli sauce, fish sauce,
    flour, spring onions, coriander and lime juice. Process for about
    1 minute until all of the ingredients are well combined.
3. Remove the chopping blade, and add half of the drained noodles.
    Stir through with a spoon.

4. Take golf-ball size amounts of the mixture and roll into patties, flattening slightly with your hands. Continue until all the mixture is used and you have 10 fishcakes.

5. Either put the fishcakes in the fridge, covered, until you are ready to use or cook them.

6. Heat a 5 mm (¼ inch) deep layer of oil in a frying pan over medium heat. Add the fishcakes in batches and cook on the first side for 1–2 minutes, then turn over and cook for a further 1–2 minutes.

7. They are cooked when they are firm to touch and have turned a lovely golden colour. If they look like they are beginning to burn, turn the heat down.

8. Serve on a bed of the remaining noodles with extra sweet chilli sauce for dipping. Add a salad or stir-fried vegetables to complete the meal, or make into fish burgers.

CHICKEN AND VEGETABLE NUGGETS

MAKES 20

Making your own chicken nuggets is obviously more time-consuming than pulling some out of the freezer, but nothing beats the satisfaction of knowing your children are eating something that is actually good for them. A little extra effort will mean you can stock your freezer with homemade nuggets for those nights you don't feel like cooking. They are also easily made gluten free.

INGREDIENTS

½ carrot, sliced

½ zucchini (courgette), peeled and sliced

400 g (14 oz) skinless chicken breast fillets, chopped

1 tablespoon garlic powder

½ tablespoon mustard powder

1 tablespoon onion powder

1 cup (125 g/4½ oz) plain (all-purpose) flour, or gluten-free plain flour

1 egg, whisked with a dash of milk

2 cups (250 g/9 oz) dry breadcrumbs: I use gluten-free corn breadcrumbs as they give a lovely crunchy texture, but panko breadcrumbs are also perfect for this recipe

cooking oil spray

LET'S PUT IT ALL TOGETHER

1. If cooking immediately, preheat the oven to 200°C (400°F) and line a baking tray with baking paper.
2. In a food processor fitted with the metal chopping blade, process the carrot and zucchini until they are finely chopped.
3. Add the chicken breast, garlic, mustard and onion powders (you can use all, some or none of these) and season with salt and pepper. Process for about 45 seconds or until the mixture starts to come together.
4. Remove the blade from the food processor. Set up a crumbing station with a bowl of flour, a bowl of the egg and milk mixture and a bowl of breadcrumbs.
5. Take tablespoon-size amounts of the chicken mixture and roughly form a nugget shape. Dust in the flour, dip in the egg mixture and roll in the breadcrumbs. Repeat until all the chicken mixture is used.
6. These can now be placed on the prepared baking tray with a spray of cooking oil and baked for 10–15 minutes until they are lightly golden and bounce back when touched. Depending on your oven you may need to turn them over halfway through the cooking time
7. To freeze, place the uncooked nuggets on a lined tray and place in the freezer. Once frozen, transfer to resealable bags and freeze. When cooking from frozen, add an extra 5 minutes baking time.

TURKISH BREAD PIZZA MELTS

SERVES 4–6

Make pizza night super-easy by substituting Turkish bread for a traditional pizza base. This is a quick and tasty twist that everyone is going to love. Pile the toppings up or keep them simple: the choice is yours.

INGREDIENTS

1 long Turkish bread loaf or focaccia

pizza sauce or pesto

Toppings: ham, pepperoni, onion, tomato, mushrooms, baby spinach, pineapple, bacon, banana, chicken, avocado

2–3 cups (250–375 g/9–13 oz) grated mozzarella cheese

LET'S PUT IT ALL TOGETHER

1. Slice the Turkish bread lengthways through the middle so that you have two lengths.
2. Lay them on a baking tray with the cut side up. Spread with the pizza sauce or pesto, then top with your chosen toppings, followed by the cheese.
3. Put the tray under the grill (broiler) and cook until the cheese is golden and melted. Cut into slices and serve.

TIP Best enjoyed on the day of making.

VEGETABLE SHREDDERS

Vegetable shredders are vibrant in colour and a perfect
way to use up all the bits and pieces of vegetables you
have hanging around in the fridge at the end of the week.
Get the kids involved in grating the vegetables.
These make a perfect quick snack or breakfast.

INGREDIENTS

2 cups grated vegetables, such as carrot, zucchini (courgette),
    potato, sweet potato, beetroot (beet) or pumpkin (squash),
    excess liquid squeezed out
1 egg
2 tablespoons plain (all-purpose) flour
olive oil, for frying

LET'S PUT IT ALL TOGETHER

1. Put the grated vegetables into a bowl, add the egg and flour and
   season with salt and pepper. Mix well to combine.
2. Heat a shallow layer of olive oil in a large non-stick frying pan
   over medium heat. The oil is hot enough when a cube of bread
   turns golden after 20 seconds. When the oil is hot enough, place
   tablespoon-size amounts of the vegetable mixture in the oil and
   flatten out into a circle. You should be able to cook four at once.
3. Cook for 1 minute before flipping to cook on the other side for
   a further minute. You want them golden on both sides. Remove
   from the pan and drain on paper towel to soak up any excess oil.
   Repeat until all of the mixture is cooked.

 TIP Best enjoyed on the day of making.

POTATO ROSTIS

MAKES 8

Quicker and easier than homemade chips, these potato rostis are super crunchy and an interesting alternative to chips when you are in a hurry. You can add other grated vegetables such as carrot, zucchini (peeled, to disguise it from the kiddos), sweet potato, onion and garlic.

INGREDIENTS

3 large sebago potatoes, peeled
¼ cup (35 g/1¼ oz) plain (all-purpose) flour
olive oil, for frying

LET'S PUT IT ALL TOGETHER

1. Grate the raw potato onto a flat baking tray, using the large holes. Make sure you carefully spread the grated potato on the tray so that it doesn't clump together.
2. Dust the flour over the potato and season with salt and pepper.
3. Heat a large non-stick frying pan with a little olive oil—enough to shallow fry the rostis. Using your hands, bring the potato together to form a golf-ball size mound. Put it in the hot oil and flatten gently with an egg flip or spatula to spread the mix out into a disc.
4. Cook for about 3 minutes on each side until golden brown. Transfer to paper towel to absorb the excess oil.
5. Repeat until all of the mixture is used.

TIPS Best enjoyed on the day of making.
Add herbs for extra seasoning.

ZUCCHINI PUFF BITES

MAKES 12

When we have had one of those days and I know the boys will be challenging at dinner time, I turn to these zucchini bites. They look a little like nuggets but are completely vegetarian and I know they will eat them.

INGREDIENTS

2 cups (270 g/9½ oz) grated zucchini (courgette), excess liquid squeezed out
½ cup (75 g/2¾ oz) self-raising flour
2 eggs
olive oil, for frying

LET'S PUT IT ALL TOGETHER

1. Put all of the ingredients except the oil in a large bowl, season with salt and pepper and mix well to combine.
2. Heat a shallow layer of olive oil in a large non-stick frying pan over medium heat. Place tablespoon-size amounts of the mixture into the oil. Don't flatten them but leave them as the mix falls.
3. Cook for 1 minute or until they are easy enough to flip. Then cook on the other side for a further minute. You will notice that they will start to puff up as they cook on the second side. They are ready when they bounce back when touched.
4. Remove from the pan and transfer to paper towel to soak up any excess oil. Repeat until all of the batter is cooked.

 TIP Best enjoyed on the day of making.

NO-KNEAD SODA BREAD

MAKES I LOAF

I love the smell of fresh bread and I normally use my breadmaker to make it. But sometimes you don't want to wait three or four hours for your bread to be ready to eat: you want it now. Soda bread is my solution when I want a little extra something with dinner or have run out of fresh bread. There is no waiting for it to rise and no kneading is required.

INGREDIENTS

4 cups (600 g/ I lb 5 oz) plain (all-purpose) flour

2 teaspoons bicarbonate of soda (baking soda)

I teaspoon salt

50 g (I ¾ oz) butter, softened

2 cups (500 ml/ I 7 fl oz) buttermilk, or mix 2 tablespoons white vinegar with 2 cups milk and set aside for 5 minutes before using

LET'S PUT IT ALL TOGETHER

1. Preheat the oven to 200°C (400°F). Line a baking tray with baking paper and set aside.
2. In a large bowl, combine the flour, bicarbonate of soda, salt and butter and use your fingertips to work the butter into the dry mix until it is all broken down.

3. Add the buttermilk (or sour milk) to the mixture and use a butter knife to stir it through until a dough starts to form. Using your hands, bring it all together to form a ball. Place the dough in the centre of the prepared baking tray. Leave it as a high dome shape and score a cross in the top.
4. Bake for 45 minutes or until it is golden and firm to touch.
5. Enjoy warm with butter (or spread cream cheese and strawberry jam on top for morning or afternoon tea).

TIP Best enjoyed on the day of making.

MARINADES FOR CHICKEN PIECES

Chicken wings and drumsticks are a budget-friendly meat that the whole family enjoys eating. I don't like to buy the pre-marinated variety. Instead, I prefer to have the fridge and pantry stocked with staples that will allow me to create my own marinades. It is not only cheaper, you also know what you are eating and can control the salt and sugar content as you wish.

Here are four of my favourite marinades.

Honey Soy
½ cup (125 ml/4 fl oz) soy sauce (low sodium)
⅓ cup (115 g/4 oz) honey
1 tablespoon crushed garlic

Satay
½ cup (140 g/5 oz) peanut butter, softened (20 seconds in the
    microwave will do the trick)
1 teaspoon curry powder
1 teaspoon crushed garlic
1 tablespoon soy sauce (low-sodium)

Plum

½ cup (165 g/5¾ oz) plum jam
½ cup (125 g/4½ oz) barbecue sauce (spicy ketchup)

Sweet and Sour

½ cup (125 g/4½ oz) tomato sauce (ketchup)
½ cup (125 ml/4 fl oz) white vinegar
½ cup (110 g/3¾ oz) sugar

LET'S PUT IT ALL TOGETHER

1. Simply combine the ingredients for each marinade in a bowl and mix well. Put the chicken pieces into the marinade and coat. Transfer to the fridge to marinate for a minimum of 1 hour before cooking. I like to coat the chicken in the marinade in the morning.

2. When ready to cook, simply put the marinated pieces onto a baking tray lined with baking paper and bake in a 200°C (400°F) oven for 1 hour.

stir-fries

Stir-fries are an easy midweek meal,
comprising four core components—sauce,
meat, vegetables and noodles—so
you can't go wrong.

BEEF AND BROCCOLI

SERVES 4

Packed full of flavour, this is an easy dinner that the whole family will enjoy. The marinating process makes the meat super-tender so that the texture is like the takeaway (take-out) variety; in fact, the whole recipe is basically a copy-cat of the takeaway dish, except that you have made it at home for half the price and you know all of the ingredients you have used.

INGREDIENTS

500 g (1 lb 2 oz) beef strips
1 onion, finely sliced
sesame oil, for stir-frying
½ head of broccoli, cut into florets
cooked rice, to serve

Marinade

1 teaspoon bicarbonate of soda (baking soda)
2 tablespoons cornflour (cornstarch)
1 tablespoon hoisin sauce
3 tablespoons soy sauce (low sodium)
1 tablespoon crushed garlic
1 teaspoon finely grated fresh ginger

Sauce

3 tablespoons oyster sauce
3 tablespoons hoisin sauce
1 tablespoon soy sauce (low sodium)
3 tablespoons sugar
1 tablespoon sesame oil

LET'S PUT IT ALL TOGETHER

1. Combine all of the marinade ingredients into a bowl and mix. Add the beef strips and mix to coat well. Transfer to the fridge and leave to marinate for 1–2 hours.
2. After the marinating time, combine all of the sauce ingredients in a bowl and set aside.
3. Using a hot wok or deep-sided frying pan, cook the onion with a little sesame oil for 1 minute.
4. Add the marinated beef strips and stir, making sure the meat is browned on all sides.
5. Add the sauce to the beef and onion and cook for 1 minute.
6. Finish off by adding the broccoli and stir-frying for a further minute.
7. Serve with the rice.

CHICKEN AND VEGETABLE SATAY NOODLES

SERVES 4–6

Satay is one of my favourite flavours and it is really easy to make your own satay sauce. Don't waste money on sauce bases, be in control of what your family is eating. You can also use this recipe to make pork or beef satay.

INGREDIENTS

olive oil, for frying

1 onion, finely sliced

500 g (1 lb 2 oz) boneless, skinless chicken thigh fillets, cut into cubes

1 tablespoon crushed garlic

1 cup (250 ml/9 fl oz) chicken stock

1 teaspoon curry powder

1 tablespoon cornflour (cornstarch)

½ cup (140 g/5 oz) crunchy peanut butter

2 cups finely sliced vegetables, such as carrot, broccoli, capsicum (peppers)

450 g (1 lb) ready-to-eat hokkien noodles

LET'S PUT IT ALL TOGETHER

1. Heat the olive oil in a large non-stick frying pan over high heat, then add the onion, chicken pieces and garlic. Cook, stirring regularly, for 5 minutes or until the chicken has started to brown.

2. Meanwhile, combine the chicken stock, curry powder and cornflour in a jug. Mix well until the cornflour is dissolved.
3. Add the peanut butter and the stock mixture to the chicken and stir well. Reduce to a simmer and cook until the sauce thickens. Add the vegetables and cook for a further 5 minutes.
4. Prepare the noodles according to the packet directions and add them to the chicken satay in the last minute.

QUICK AND EASY CHICKEN, VEGETABLE AND NOODLE STIR-FRY

SERVES 4

Dinner cooked and on the table in 10 minutes. Sounds too good to be true, but it isn't. I am using the crunchy salad mix you can find in the ready-made salad section of your local supermarket, which means no chopping. Simply throw everything together and let it cook.

INGREDIENTS

250 g (9 oz) long life noodles, such as Chang's
2 tablespoons sesame oil
4 boneless, skinless chicken thigh fillets, diced
½ × 260 g (9¼ oz) packet Crunchy Salad Kit
3 tablespoons tamari oyster sauce
3 tablespoons sweet chilli sauce
1 tablespoon soy sauce (low sodium)

LET'S PUT IT ALL TOGETHER

1. Put the long life noodles into a large heatproof bowl and cover with boiling water. Set aside for 5 minutes to soften.
2. Meanwhile, heat the sesame oil in a large frying pan over high heat. It will heat quickly. Add the chicken thighs and cook, moving them around, until the chicken is lightly browned.

3. Add the crunchy salad mix and stir through. Allow to soften slightly.
4. The noodles should now be soft, so separate them with a fork. Drain off the water and add the noodles to the frying pan.
5. Add the tamari oyster sauce, sweet chilli sauce and soy sauce to the frying pan and toss all the ingredients really well to combine. Allow to cook for 1 further minute, then remove from the heat and serve.

TIP If you can't purchase the Crunchy Salad Kit, substitute with shredded cabbage, grated carrot, sliced onion and celery to the same quantity.

GREENS AND SOBA NOODLES

SERVES 2 AS A SIDE DISH

This is a wonderful dish to make when you want to eat something full of nutritional goodness. It's so easy to enjoy late at night after a hectic day because it is light, yet filling.

INGREDIENTS

olive oil, for frying

2 tablespoons crushed garlic

1 large head of broccoli, cut into florets

6 large silverbeet (Swiss chard) leaves, shredded, or 3 cups (135 g/4¾ oz) baby spinach leaves

dried garlic and onion flakes (found in the herb section of the supermarket) (optional)

1 × 90 g (3¼ oz) bundle soba buckwheat noodles, cooked

sesame seeds, to garnish

LET'S PUT IT ALL TOGETHER

1. Heat the olive oil in a frying pan over high heat.
2. Add the garlic and broccoli and cook, stirring constantly, for 3 minutes.
3. Add the silverbeet and reduce the heat to low. Keep stirring for 1 minute until it wilts.
4. Add the dried garlic and onion flakes, if using, and season with salt and pepper. Toss to combine.

5. Remove from the heat. Add the soba noodles (prepared according to the packet instructions) and mix through.
6. Finish with a sprinkling of sesame seeds.

TIP Add a dash of soy sauce or sweet soy sauce (kecap manis) at the end.

EASY SINGAPORE-STYLE NOODLES

SERVES 4–6

The flavours of this meal are spot on: you will think twice next time you want to order Singapore noodles from a Chinese restaurant now that you know how easy they are to make. It's also a lot cheaper and quicker; this meal will be on the table in less than 15 minutes.

INGREDIENTS

150 g (5½ oz) dry vermicelli noodles
sesame oil, for frying
2 eggs, lightly whisked with a little salt and pepper
5 boneless, skinless chicken thigh fillets, cut into strips
1 × 500 g (1 lb 2oz) packet frozen Thai-style stir-fry vegetables
1 teaspoon curry powder
1 teaspoon fish sauce
3 tablespoons sweet chilli sauce
1 teaspoon soy sauce (low sodium)
½ cup (80 g/2¾ oz) cashew nuts (optional)
thinly sliced spring onions (scallions), to serve (optional)

LET'S PUT IT ALL TOGETHER

1. Put the noodles into a bowl of hot water and set aside. They will soften by the time you are ready to add them to the wok. Drain before adding to the other ingredients.

2. Turn the electric wok on to setting 10 (or a non-stick fry pan over a high heat) and allow to heat for 30 seconds. Add a little oil. Pour in the whisked eggs and move them around in the wok until light and fluffy. Remove from the wok and transfer to a plate to use later. Toss the chicken strips into the wok and stir-fry, tossing regularly, until lightly golden.

3. Move the chicken to one side of the wok and add the frozen vegetables to the other side. Allow to heat for 30 seconds and then stir through the chicken.

4. Add the curry powder, fish sauce, sweet chilli sauce and soy sauce, then season with salt and pepper. Stir through. Add the cashew nuts, if using, and finally the softened vermicelli noodles. Toss to combine. Turn the wok off.

5. Cut the cooked egg into strips.

6. Serve by laying the egg strips on top of the chicken and noodle mixture, along with a sprinkling of spring onions if you like.

SESAME NOODLES

SERVES 4

....

This is such a simple and comforting dish. These noodles
are likely to be favoured as teenager food—a better
alternative to the two-minute noodles you buy with their
own seasoning (they are also full of more flavour).
Make a big batch and store leftovers in the fridge
for up to three days.

....

INGREDIENTS

400 g (14 oz) ready-to-eat Singapore noodles
1 tablespoon crushed garlic
¼ cup (60 ml/2 fl oz) soy sauce (low sodium)
2 tablespoons sugar
3 tablespoons sesame oil
2 tablespoons olive oil
2 spring onions (scallions), white part only, finely sliced
finely chopped small red chilli, to taste (optional)

LET'S PUT IT ALL TOGETHER

1. Heat the noodles by soaking in water, according to the packet
   instructions.
2. Mix together the garlic, soy, sugar, sesame oil and olive oil in a
   small bowl.

3. Once the noodles have loosened and heated through, drain the water. Transfer the noodles to a wok or frying pan over high heat, pour in the sauce mixture and cook, stirring, for 2 minutes.
4. Top with the spring onion and chilli (if using).

 **TIP** This noodle base is so versatile. You can add chicken or beef for a complete meal; simply cook the meat before adding the noodles.

CHICKEN AND CASHEW NUTS

SERVES 4–6

In the same amount of time that it will take to go to
your local takeaway (take-out) store and pick up
a meal, you can have this healthy dish on the table.
Save money and time and make it at home.

INGREDIENTS

sesame oil, for cooking

4 skinless chicken breast fillets, diced

2 carrots, grated

200 g (7 oz) snow peas (mangetout)

1 cup (155 g/5½ oz) salted cashew nuts

cooked rice, to serve

Sauce

1 cup (250 ml/9 fl oz) of water

2 teaspoons chicken stock powder

½ teaspoon finely grated fresh ginger

1 teaspoon crushed garlic

2 tablespoons hoisin sauce

2 tablespoons cornflour (cornstarch)

2 tablespoons honey

LET'S PUT IT ALL TOGETHER

1. Put some oil in a hot wok or non-stick frying pan. Add the chicken
    pieces and cook, stirring, until browned on all sides. Combine all
    of the sauce ingredients in a bowl or jug and whisk together until
    the cornflour is dissolved.

2. Once the chicken has browned, pour in the sauce and stir until the sauce thickens. Reduce to a simmer, cover with a lid and cook for 5 minutes.
3. Turn off the heat, add the carrot, snow peas and cashews and stir through.
4. Serve with the cooked rice.

Dinners

What's for dinner? This would have to be the most asked question in any home. Instead of cringing at the thought of dinner, just take your pick from these recipes that are easy, frugal and, most importantly, delicious.

SAUSAGES

Everyone loves sausages—I am talking about the kind the butcher makes with minced (ground) beef, pork or chicken in an edible skin, rather than spiced and cured meats—because they are easy to cook and eat. Here are our favourite ways to turn them into a balanced meal.

HEALTHIER CURRIED SAUSAGES

SERVES 4

Load this dish up with vegetables to take it from an ordinary meal to a healthier alternative. This dish serves four: simply double it if you want leftovers or have a larger family to feed.

INGREDIENTS

6 butchers' sausages
olive oil, for frying
1 onion, thinly sliced
2 garlic cloves, thinly sliced
2 teaspoons curry powder (or adjust to your taste)
1 carrot, thinly sliced
1 cup (125 g/4½ oz) cauliflower florets or chopped zucchini (courgette)
½ red capsicum (pepper), deseeded and thinly sliced
1 cup (250 ml/9 fl oz) beef stock
cooked rice, to serve

LET'S PUT IT ALL TOGETHER

1. In a large saucepan of hot water, parboil the sausages for approximately 5 minutes, remove from the water and slice into discs.
2. In a frying pan, heat some olive oil and sauté the onion and garlic until softened.
3. Add the curry powder to the pan and cook, stirring, until aromatic.

4. Add the sausages and remaining vegetables and stir to coat with the curry powder, then cook for 5 minutes.
5. Add the stock and reduce to a simmer for 10 minutes or until the vegetables soften.
6. Season with pepper.
7. Serve with cooked rice, such as brown rice, to add extra fibre to this dish.

CHEESE AND TOMATO SAUSAGE PASTA BAKE WITH ADDED GREEN VEGETABLES

SERVES 6–8

This recipe is a great after-work meal: a few steps of preparation and then simply leave it in the oven until it's done. Try this dish with lamb and rosemary sausages and it won't disappoint.

INGREDIENTS

400 g (14 oz) penne pasta

1 zucchini (courgette), chopped

500 g (1 lb 2 oz) butchers' sausages

1 × 575 g (1 lb 4½ oz) jar Cheese & Tomato Pasta Bake, or other ready-made pasta sauce or similar

2 handfuls of baby spinach leaves

1 cup (100 g/4 oz) grated tasty cheddar cheese

LET'S PUT IT ALL TOGETHER

1. Preheat the oven to 200°C (400°F). Set a large saucepan of water on the stove and bring to the boil, add the pasta and diced zucchini and cook until just al dente. You want the pasta to be a little undercooked as it will finish cooking in the oven.
2. Sear the sausages in a hot frying pan while the pasta cooks. You just want to brown the outside. Remove from the pan, allow to cool slightly, then slice into discs.

3. When the pasta and zucchini are ready, drain and return to the warm saucepan. Add the pasta sauce, sliced sausages and baby spinach leaves and mix well to combine.
4. Pour into a baking dish and sprinkle with the grated cheese. Bake in the oven for 20 minutes.

BAKED SAUSAGES, SALAMI AND POTATO

SERVES 4–6

This is a simple one-pan meal: throw everything
in raw and pop it into the oven to cook.
While it's cooking you are free to do other things,
like wrangling bath time.

INGREDIENTS

3 (desiree) potatoes, thinly sliced
I carrot, thinly sliced
I onion, thinly sliced
100 g (3½ oz) mild salami, sliced
½ teaspoon each dried rosemary and oregano, for sprinkling
8 butchers' sausages
finely chopped fresh flat-leaf (Italian) parsley, for sprinkling
grated tasty cheddar cheese (optional)
garlic bread and green salad, to serve

LET'S PUT IT ALL TOGETHER

1. Preheat the oven to 160°C (315°F).
2. In a baking dish, make a layer of half of the sliced potato followed by a layer of half of the carrot, onion and salami. Sprinkle with the rosemary and oregano, season with salt and pepper, then add four of the sausages.
3. Repeat with the remaining potato, carrot, onion, salami, dried herbs and sausages. Scatter with the parsley, then add ¾ cup (185 ml/6 fl oz) of water and bake, uncovered, for 20 minutes.

4. Cover the dish with a lid or some foil and bake for another 30–40 minutes until the vegetables have softened.
5. Remove the lid, sprinkle on the cheese, if using, turn the oven up to 200°C (400°F) and bake for an additional 10 minutes to give the potatoes some colour.
6. Enjoy with garlic bread and a leafy salad.

TIP Best eaten on the day it is made.

SAUSAGE AND VEGETABLE HOTPOT

SERVES 4–6

This is a real family-friendly, hearty meal that is sure to keep tummies satisfied during the cooler weather. It's budget friendly and can easily be adapted to suit other meats, such as chicken thighs and cheaper cuts of beef.
Use the base ingredients of this recipe—bacon, onion, garlic, tomato purée, stock and chickpeas—and experiment with different combinations of meat and vegetables.

INGREDIENTS

500 g (1 lb 2 oz) butchers' sausages
1 onion, thinly sliced
1 tablespoon crushed garlic
3 bacon rashers, rind removed, chopped
1 red capsicum (pepper), deseeded and chopped
1 carrot, chopped into cubes
1 cup (140 g/5 oz) frozen peas
400 g (14 oz) tin chickpeas, rinsed and drained
400 ml (14 fl oz) tomato purée
1 cup (250 ml/9 fl oz) chicken stock
2 cups pasta, such as penne, or crusty bread (optional)

LET'S PUT IT ALL TOGETHER

1. Preheat the oven to 150°C (300°F).
2. In a frying pan over medium–high heat, fry the sausages, onion, garlic and bacon. Cook until lightly golden, while you are preparing the vegetables.
3. In an ovenproof dish with a lid, put the vegetables and add the sausage mixture from the pan, followed by the chickpeas.
4. Pour in the tomato purée and chicken stock, then mix gently to combine all of the ingredients.
5. Cover with the lid and bake for 2–3 hours. If you wish, stir through the pasta and 1 cup (250 ml/9 fl oz) of water 30 minutes before finishing.
6. If not adding pasta, serve with some crusty bread to soak up the juices.

ONE-POT DEVILLED SAUSAGES WITH MACARONI

SERVES 4–6

If you haven't made devilled sausages before, the flavour is somewhat tangy and sweet all at the same time. There is no heat (chilli) in this dish at all, although you could add some chilli powder if you like. I try to make one-pot meals because I hate washing dishes and I like things to be easy in the evening, so I add macaroni and carrots to the dish to complete it.

INGREDIENTS

8 butchers' sausages (pork, chicken or beef)
1 tablespoon crushed garlic
2 onions, thinly sliced
1 tablespoon olive oil
1 apple, cored and thinly sliced
1 carrot, thinly sliced
400 g (14 oz) tin chopped tomatoes
¼ cup (60 ml/2 fl oz) tomato sauce (ketchup)
¼ cup (60 ml/2 fl oz) barbecue sauce (spicy ketchup)
1 tablespoon brown sugar
1 tablespoon white vinegar
300 ml (10½ fl oz) chicken stock
1 cup (155 g/5½ oz) macaroni

LET'S PUT IT ALL TOGETHER

1. In a heavy-based saucepan, cook the sausages, garlic and onion with the olive oil over medium heat until the sausages are browned and the onion has softened.
2. Add the apple and carrot and cook for a further 1 minute. Add the tomatoes. Use the empty tin to mix up the tomato and barbecue sauces, brown sugar and vinegar; stir, then pour into the pan, followed by the chicken stock. Mix well.
3. Turn the heat down to low and add the macaroni. Cover with the lid and allow to simmer for 15–20 minutes. Stir halfway through the cooking time to make sure the macaroni doesn't stick to the bottom of the pan.

SAUSAGE AND BACON STROGANOFF

SERVES 4–6

This meal has all the flavour of a traditional stroganoff.
It is a really frugal family meal that will have everyone
coming back for seconds and licking their bowls clean.

INGREDIENTS

8 thick beef butchers' sausages
1 tablespoon olive oil
4 bacon rashers, rind removed, chopped
1 onion, chopped
1 tablespoon crushed garlic
8 button mushrooms, sliced
¼ cup (60 ml/2 fl oz) Worcestershire sauce
2 tablespoons tomato paste
1 cup (250 ml/9 fl oz) chicken stock
⅓ cup (85 g/3 oz) sour cream
finely chopped fresh flat-leaf (Italian) parsley, to serve (optional)

LET'S PUT IT ALL TOGETHER

1. Heat a large non-stick frying pan over medium–high heat. Add
   the sausages and cook for 5–10 minutes until browned on all
   sides. Remove from the pan.
2. Put the olive oil in the frying pan and sauté the bacon, onion and
   garlic until soft. Add the mushrooms and cook, stirring regularly,
   for a further 5 minutes. Stir through the Worcestershire sauce,
   tomato paste and chicken stock.

3. Reduce to a simmer and cook for 5 minutes. Slice the sausages and add to the pan, cooking for another 3 minutes. Stir through the sour cream and remove from the heat.

4. Top with a sprinkling of parsley, if you like. Enjoy with rice, pasta or crusty bread.

MINCED (GROUND) MEAT

Whether it is beef, chicken, pork, veal or turkey, minced (ground) meat shows up regularly in our house. The boys' favourite meal is spaghetti bolognese and, if I let them, they would eat it every night of the week.

HIDDEN VEGETABLE BOLOGNESE

SERVES 6–8

This is the famous spaghetti bolognese that my boys can't get enough of. You can make a double batch and freeze the bolognese sauce in freezer bags, ready for a night when you don't feel like cooking.

INGREDIENTS

olive oil, for frying
1 onion, finely chopped
2 garlic cloves, finely chopped
500 g (1 lb 2 oz) minced (ground) pork or beef
1 carrot, grated
1 zucchini (courgette), grated
1 small red capsicum (pepper), finely chopped
3 mushrooms, finely chopped
420 g (15 oz) tin tomato soup
1 cup (250 ml/9 fl oz) chicken stock
chopped fresh flat-leaf (Italian) parsley, to serve
cooked spaghetti, to serve
grated parmesan cheese, to serve (optional)

LET'S PUT IT ALL TOGETHER

1. Set a large saucepan over medium–high heat and add a splash of olive oil. Add the onion and garlic, stir and cook until softened.
2. Add the meat and season with salt and pepper, stirring until browned.

3. Add the carrot, zucchini, capsicum and mushrooms. Mix through and cook, stirring regularly, for a further 5 minutes until the vegetables start to soften.
4. Add the tomato soup, chicken stock and 1 cup (250 ml/9 fl oz) of water to the pan.
5. Reduce to a low simmer and allow to cook for 1 hour with the lid on, stirring occasionally.
6. Add the fresh parsley and serve with the spaghetti. Top with the cheese if you like.

SPAGHETTI PIE WITH A CREAMY TOP

SERVES 8–10

Leftover spaghetti bolognese: want to make something different with it? Then this spaghetti pie is what you are looking for. The creamy top transforms it from just spaghetti bolognese in a dish to a meal you can easily feed a crowd with.

INGREDIENTS

360 g (12¾ oz) cooked spaghetti
1 quantity of Hidden Vegetable Bolognese (see pages 132–3)
250 g (9 oz) light cream cheese
200 g (7 oz) light sour cream
2 cups (200 g/7 oz) grated light cheddar cheese

LET'S PUT IT ALL TOGETHER

1. Preheat the oven to 200°C (400°F). Combine the cooked spaghetti with the bolognese sauce and mix well. Pour into a large baking dish.
2. In a medium bowl, combine the cream cheese and sour cream. Mix well, then spread over the top of the bolognese mixture. Finish with the grated cheese. Bake for approximately 15 minutes until the creamy cheese layer starts to bubble and turn a lovely golden colour.
3. Cut sections out to serve.

CHICKEN AND BACON BALLS WITH HIDDEN VEGETABLES

MAKES 30+

This recipe for chicken and bacon balls with hidden vegetables is a tasty family-friendly meal. They are easy to make, include hidden vegetables and are bite-size for little mouths.
There is the added bonus that the meat mixture can be made into sausage rolls—and we know everyone loves sausage rolls.
These are perfect for the school lunchbox, an easy dinner or to take on a picnic.

INGREDIENTS
cooking oil spray
1 onion, roughly chopped
2 carrots, roughly chopped
1 zucchini (courgette), roughly chopped (peeled if you wish to disguise it even more)
200 g (7 oz) rindless streaky bacon (I use D'Orsogna), chopped
500 g (1 lb 2 oz) minced (ground) chicken
1 tablespoon crushed garlic
plain (all-purpose) flour, for coating
dipping sauces, such as barbecue sauce (spicy ketchup), tomato sauce (ketchup) and garlic aioli, to serve

LET'S PUT IT ALL TOGETHER

1. Preheat the oven to 200°C (400°F). Spray a baking dish with cooking oil and set aside.
2. Using a food processor or a Thermomix, process the onion, carrot and zucchini until finely chopped.
3. Put the streaky bacon into a frying pan over high heat and cook until lightly browned and the flavour is released. Add the bacon to the vegetable mixture and process for 10 seconds.
4. Add the chicken and garlic and season with salt and pepper. Process on low speed to just combine with the other ingredients. Be careful not to overprocess it.
5. Put some flour on your hands and roll tablespoon-size amounts of the mixture to form a ball shape. Place in the prepared baking dish.
6. Repeat until all the mixture is used.
7. Spray the chicken balls with cooking spray and bake for 20 minutes or until lightly golden and they bounce back when touched. Serve with the dipping sauce or sauces of your choice.

LAMB AND FETA MEATBALLS

MAKES 60+

This recipe makes approximately 60 meatballs, giving you enough to enjoy on the day of making and enough to freeze in batches for meals in the coming weeks. The meatballs are packed full of flavour and are perfect for eating on their own, covered in pasta sauce or in a bread roll with salad for lunch.

INGREDIENTS

1.5 kg (3 lb 5 oz) minced (ground) lamb
200 g (7 oz) Greek-style feta cheese, crumbled
1 tablespoon dried rosemary
¾ cup (85 g/3 oz) dry breadcrumbs
1 carrot, grated
1 onion, chopped
2 tablespoons crushed garlic
¼ cup (60 ml/2 fl oz) barbecue sauce (spicy ketchup)
olive oil, for frying

LET'S PUT IT ALL TOGETHER

1. In a large bowl, combine all of the ingredients, using your hands give it a good working. Continue to work the mix for a further minute.
2. Take tablespoon-size amounts and roll into meatballs. Wet your hands when rolling as it makes it easier to work into a ball and keeps the mixture from sticking to your hands.

3. If you are going to freeze them, place a single layer in labelled resealable plastic bags. Freeze flat. These meatballs can be frozen for up to three months.

4. If you're not freezing them, you can make them in the morning and store them on a plate covered with plastic wrap in the fridge, ready to cook in the evening.

5. In a frying pan, heat enough olive oil for shallow frying. Heat the oven to 180°C (350°F). Line a baking tray with baking paper and set aside. When the oil is hot, put the meatballs into the frying pan and cook, turning occasionally, until they are golden.

6. Remove from the pan and place on the prepared baking tray. Repeat until the desired amount is cooked.

7. Transfer the tray with the meatballs to the oven and cook for a further 10 minutes. Finishing off the cooking process in the oven prevents the meatballs from burning in the frying pan.

BEEF AND VEGETABLE MEATBALLS

MAKES 24–30

One of our family's favourite meatballs, these are made
with ingredients that are fridge and pantry staples and,
again, are a perfect smuggler of vegetables for fussy eaters.

INGREDIENTS

1 carrot, chopped
1 zucchini (courgette), chopped
1 onion, chopped
2 garlic cloves, peeled
500 g (1 lb 2 oz) minced (ground) beef
1 teaspoon dried oregano
1 egg
¾ cup (85 g/3 oz) dry breadcrumbs
olive oil, for frying
plain (all-purpose) flour, for rolling

LET'S PUT IT ALL TOGETHER

1. Using a food processor fitted with the metal chopping blade,
   process the carrot, zucchini, onion and garlic for 20 seconds
   until they are all chopped into small pieces. If you don't have a
   food processor you can simply grate the vegetables.
2. In a large bowl, combine the meat, oregano, egg and breadcrumbs, then season with salt and pepper and add the
   vegetable mixture. Work well with your hands to combine all
   the ingredients.

3. Roll tablespoon-size amounts of the mix into balls. Place on a plate. Repeat until all are done.
4. Refrigerate for 30 minutes or until you are ready to use them.
5. In a frying pan, heat enough olive oil for shallow frying. Pre-heat the oven to 180°C (350°F). Line a baking tray with baking paper and set aside. Meanwhile, start to roll the meatballs gently in the flour. When the oil is hot, put the meatballs, in batches, into the frying pan and cook, turning occasionally, until they are golden.
6. Remove from the pan and place on the prepared baking tray. Repeat until all the meatballs are cooked.
7. Transfer the tray with the meatballs to the oven and cook for a further 10 minutes. Finishing off the cooking process in the oven prevents the meatballs from burning in the frying pan.

BAKED SWEET PORK MEATBALLS

MAKES 40+

Sweet pork meatballs are baked in the oven in a hoisin sauce. They make an ideal appetiser, or a main meal served with steamed vegetables and rice.

INGREDIENTS

Meatballs

500 g (1 lb 2 oz) minced (ground) pork

1 carrot, grated

1 onion, diced

2 tablespoons crushed garlic

½ cup (55 g/2 oz) dry breadcrumbs

Sauce

½ cup (125 ml/4 fl oz) hoisin sauce

¼ cup (60 ml/2 fl oz) soy sauce (low sodium)

½ cup (125 ml/4 fl oz) water

1 tablespoon finely grated fresh ginger

LET'S PUT IT ALL TOGETHER

1. Preheat the oven to 200°C (400°F).
2. Put all of the meatball ingredients into a bowl and use your hands to work the mixture together. Alternatively, use a food processor.
3. Roll tablespoon-size amounts of the meatball mixture and place in an ovenproof dish. Repeat until all the mixture is rolled.

4. Mix the ingredients for the sauce together, add the water and pour over the meatballs. Toss the meatballs in the sauce to coat all sides. You can leave these in the fridge until you are ready to bake them.
5. Cover the dish with a lid or some foil and bake for 15 minutes.
6. Uncover and bake for another 10 minutes. They are ready when the meatballs bounce back when touched.

MEDITERRANEAN CHICKEN PATTIES

MAKES 10–12 PATTIES

These are a real crowd-pleaser. They are easy to prepare with the help of a food processor and are even quicker to be demolished on the plate. They are dairy free, egg free and gluten free (if you cook without coating in breadcrumbs or use gluten-free crumbs). Enjoy with a side salad or in a burger.

INGREDIENTS

1 zucchini (courgette), peeled
½ red capsicum (pepper), cut into 2 cm (¾ inch) strips
½ onion
500 g (1 lb 2 oz) minced (ground) chicken
½ cup (100 g/3½ oz) corn kernels
1 tablespoon dried oregano
1 tablespoon dried basil
dry breadcrumbs, for coating
olive oil, for frying
Greek yoghurt, to serve
sweet potato chips, to serve
leafy salad, to serve

LET'S PUT IT ALL TOGETHER

1. Using a food processor fitted with the grating blade, pass through the zucchini, capsicum and onion. Alternatively, you can grate the zucchini and onion by hand and finely chop the capsicum.
2. Remove the grating blade and fit the plastic mixing blade. Add the chicken, corn kernels and dried herbs, and season with salt and pepper to taste.
3. Replace the lid of the food processor and mix on low for 30 seconds to combine. Or combine by hand in a large mixing bowl.
4. Transfer to a bowl, cover and store in the fridge for 30 minutes before using.
5. Put some breadcrumbs on a plate and take golf-ball size amounts of the chicken mix (it will be quite wet) and form into patties, then coat in the breadcrumbs.
6. Only make the quantity that will fit into the frying pan at one time.
7. Put some olive oil into a large frying pan over medium heat and cook the patties, turning frequently so as not to burn them. Transfer to paper towel to drain any excess oil.
8. Repeat until all the chicken mix in used.
9. Serve with a dollop of Greek yoghurt, some oven-baked sweet potato chips and a salad.

HOMEMADE HAMBURGER PATTIES

MAKES 8 LARGE PATTIES

I love making homemade burgers. You can make them as big or as little as you like and they are a great way to get salad into non-salad-eating members of the family. You can use your hands to combine the mix; however, I prefer to use a food processor as it makes light work of it and I don't get cold, sticky hands.

INGREDIENTS

Cooking oil spray

Patties

500 g (1 lb 2 oz) minced (ground) beef

½ onion, finely chopped

1 tablespoon crushed garlic

1 egg

2 tablespoons barbecue sauce (spicy ketchup)

¾ cup (85 g/3 oz) dry breadcrumbs

1 tablespoon dried parsley or finely chopped fresh flat-leaf (Italian) parsley

1 tablespoon wholegrain mustard

LET'S PUT IT ALL TOGETHER

1. Put all of the patty ingredients in a food processor fitted with the plastic mixing blade. Process on high for 1 minute, making sure everything is mixed really well.

2. Roll into burger patties.
3. Spray a large frying pan with desired amount of cooking spray, place on the stove on medium heat. Put the desired amount of patties into the hot pan. Allow to cook, turning every minute or so. This will ensure they cook all the way through without burning. Depending on the thickness of the patties, they will take 10 minutes to cook or cook until they bounce back when touched.
4. Serve with your favourite accompaniments. We love cooked egg, cheese, lettuce, tomato, mayonnaise, avocado, sliced beetroot (beet), pineapple rings and tomato sauce (ketchup).

ASIAN-INSPIRED PORK PATTIES

MAKES 8 LARGE PATTIES

Enjoy the flavours of Asia in a versatile patty the whole family will love. Enjoy with a noodle salad or serve in a bread roll with a crunchy salad.

INGREDIENTS

olive oil, for frying
finely chopped small red chilli, to taste (optional)

Patties

500 g (1 lb 2 oz) minced (ground) pork
1 carrot, grated
½ zucchini (courgette), grated
½ onion, finely chopped
1 teaspoon crushed fresh ginger
1 tablespoon finely chopped fresh coriander (cilantro)
1 tablespoon fish sauce

LET'S PUT IT ALL TOGETHER

1. In a food processor fitted with the plastic mixing blade, combine all of the patty ingredients. Add chilli to taste if you like. Process on high for 1 minute, making sure everything is mixed really well. This helps to work the proteins in the meat and means that you don't need to add any eggs or breadcrumbs.
2. Form into medium-size patties about 2 cm (¾ inch) thick and cook in batches in a non-stick frying pan over medium heat with a little oil. Cook for 2 minutes on each side, turning regularly to avoid burning.

SAVOURY MINCE

SERVES 6–8

Budget-friendly and extremely versatile, this is a dish the whole family will enjoy. Serve on a baked potato, spoon onto toast or eat it straight from the bowl.

INGREDIENTS

olive oil, for frying
1 onion, chopped
1 tablespoon crushed garlic
500 g (1 lb 2 oz) minced (ground) beef
1 large carrot, grated
2 cups (150 g/5½ oz) shredded white cabbage
1 cup (250 ml/9 fl oz) beef stock
1 tablespoon barbecue sauce (spicy ketchup)
1 tablespoon cornflour (cornstarch)

LET'S PUT IT ALL TOGETHER

1. In a large non-stick frying pan, heat a splash of olive oil and sauté the onion and garlic until softened.
2. Add the beef and use a wooden spoon to break it down into smaller pieces, cooking until browned. Add the carrot and cabbage and mix through.
3. In a bowl or jug, combine the stock, barbecue sauce and cornflour, making sure the cornflour dissolves completely. Pour into the frying pan. Simmer for 10 minutes or until the liquid reduces and thickens.

KOREAN BEEF

SERVES 4–6

A twist on the traditional Korean beef recipe that requires beef strips, this one is quick, frugal and super-addictive. Serve with brown rice and vegetables, and you have a meal everyone will enjoy.

INGREDIENTS

1 tablespoon olive oil
2 tablespoons crushed garlic
500 g (1 lb 2 oz) minced (ground) beef
⅓ cup (60 g/2¼ oz) brown sugar
¼ cup (60 ml/2 fl oz) soy sauce (low sodium)
½ teaspoon ground ginger

LET'S PUT IT ALL TOGETHER

1. In a large non-stick frying pan over high heat, put the olive oil and allow to heat. Add the garlic and cook, stirring, for 30 seconds. Add the beef and cook for about 5 minutes until browned, making sure to break the mince up with a spoon as it cooks.
2. In a small bowl, mix together the brown sugar, soy sauce and ground ginger. Pour over the mince and stir to combine. Reduce to a simmer and allow to cook for a further 2 minutes or until the mince is cooked through.

LAMB KOFTA

SERVES 4–6

My kids go crazy for anything on a stick and these lamb koftas are no exception. You can make them in the morning and have them waiting in the fridge to cook in the evening.

INGREDIENTS

olive oil, for brushing
leafy salad, to serve

Kofta

500 g (1 lb 2 oz) minced (ground) lamb
1 onion, chopped
2 tablespoons crushed garlic
2 teaspoons ground ginger
2 tablespoons chopped fresh flat-leaf (Italian) parsley
2 tablespoons chopped mint

LET'S PUT IT ALL TOGETHER

1. If using bamboo skewers, soak them in water for at least 10 minutes to prevent them from burning during cooking. In a large bowl, place all of the kofta ingredients and use your hands to ensure they are well combined. Alternatively, put the ingredients into the bowl of a food processor fitted with the plastic mixing blade and process gently until combined.

2. Divide the mixture into 8–12 portions and wrap a portion of the mixture around the top half of a skewer, forming an oval shape. Repeat until all the mixture is used.

3. Store the kofta kebabs in the fridge on a covered plate or cook immediately. Brush with a little olive oil and grill them on a barbecue or fry them in a non-stick frying pan over medium heat. Cook for 3–5 minutes on each side until browned and the kofta bounce back when touched.
4. Serve with a salad.

CHEESY CORN AND BEEF QUESADILLAS

MAKES 5

This is a really fun dinner—or lunch—that is a big hit with everyone. Why not make double the amount of meat and freeze it, ready for a night when you want a quick meal.

INGREDIENTS

250 g (9 oz) minced (ground) beef
2 tablespoons Taco Seasoning (see page 331)
½ cup (125 g/4½ oz) tinned chopped tomatoes
½ cup (100 g/3½ oz) corn kernels
10 tortilla wraps
I cup (125 g/4½ oz) grated mozzarella cheese

LET'S PUT IT ALL TOGETHER

1. To make the beef filling, simply cook the beef in a large non-stick frying pan over high heat until browned, making sure to break the mince down into smaller pieces. Add the taco seasoning, diced tomatoes and corn kernels and stir through. Reduce to a simmer and cook for 5 minutes. Remove from the pan.

2. Wipe the frying pan with paper towel and heat over medium heat. Place one tortilla in the pan and top with a fifth of the beef mixture and a sprinkling of mozzarella cheese, then place another tortilla on top. Squash down. Cook until the bottom tortilla starts to brown lightly, then gently flip and cook on the other side until the cheese melts. Slide out of the pan and repeat with the remaining ingredients.

HOMEMADE SKINLESS CHICKEN AND APRICOT SAUSAGES

MAKES 20

Making your own skinless sausages is really easy with the help of a food processor. In these sausages I have been able to smuggle vegetables, which makes them perfect for fussy eaters.

INGREDIENTS

15 dried apricots
½ zucchini (courgette), peeled and chopped
1 carrot, chopped
500 g (1 lb 2 oz) minced (ground) chicken
½ cup (55 g/2 oz) dry breadcrumbs
1 teaspoon chicken stock powder
olive oil, for frying

LET'S PUT IT ALL TOGETHER

1. In a food processor, process the apricots until they are finely chopped. Add the zucchini and carrot and process until finely chopped as well.
2. Add the chicken, breadcrumbs and chicken stock powder to the food processor. Process until well combined (approximately 1 minute). Chicken is high in protein so it doesn't need any egg to bind it.

3. Heat a layer of olive oil in a large frying pan over medium heat (not high, as they will burn easily). Wet your hands slightly, then take golf-ball size amounts and roll between your palms until you form a finger-size sausage. Place in the heated frying pan and continue rolling the rest of the mix. Cook the sausages for approximately 5–8 minutes, turning regularly to avoid burning, until cooked through.
4. Serve with pasta, salad, roast vegetables, mashed potato (or whatever you like, really).

TIP You can prepare the mixture in the morning and store it in an airtight container until you are ready to roll and cook in the evening.

BEEF

Whether you are using strips, steak,
roast or stewing beef, here are new ways
your family can enjoy eating it.

BEEF AND VEGETABLE CASSEROLE WITH HERB DUMPLINGS

SERVES 4–6

Casseroles are a great way to make the most of cheap cuts of meat and use up bits and pieces in the fridge. This beef and vegetable casserole hits the spot, especially with the addition of the herb dumplings.

INGREDIENTS

1 tablespoon olive oil
1 onion, chopped
4 garlic cloves, sliced
1.2 kg (2 lb 11 oz) gravy (casserole) beef, cut into chunks
4 bacon rashers, rind removed, chopped
2 tablespoons plain (all-purpose) flour
6 button mushrooms, sliced
2 carrots, sliced
2 zucchini (courgettes), sliced
2 cups (500 ml/ 17 fl oz) beef stock
1 cup (250 ml/9 fl oz) red wine (or omit and substitute with
    another cup of beef stock)
2 thyme sprigs
3 dried bay leaves

DUMPLINGS

2 cups (300 g/ 10½ oz) self-raising flour
2 teaspoons chopped fresh or dried herbs of choice
50 g (1¾ oz) butter, chopped and softened
¾ cup (185 ml/6 fl oz) milk

LET'S PUT IT ALL TOGETHER

1. Preheat the oven to 180°C (350°F).
2. Set a flameproof casserole dish over a medium-high heat and add the olive oil. Add the onion and garlic along with the beef. Cook, stirring, until the beef browns.
3. Add the bacon and cook for 3 minutes.
4. Add the plain flour and stir to combine.
5. Add the mushrooms, carrot and zucchini (or your favourite vegetables) and stir through.
6. Add the beef stock and red wine (if using), along with the thyme and bay leaves. Season with salt and pepper. Stir well, scraping the bottom of the dish to move any flour that has stuck.
7. Cover and transfer to the oven, cooking for 1 ½ hours.
8. To make the dumplings, put the flour, herbs and butter in a large bowl. Use your fingers to rub the butter through the flour.
9. Add the milk gradually, stirring with a knife to form a soft ball of dough. Don't overwork the dough: treat it like a scone mix. Divide the dough and roll it into about 20 small balls.
10. Remove the casserole dish from the oven and put the dumplings gently on top of the beef mixture.
11. Return the uncovered dish to the oven and increase the temperature to 200°C (400°F). Cook for 20 minutes or until the dumplings start to brown.

BEEF STROGANOFF

SERVES 4–6

This is a true family classic that I never tire of.
I like to add a few extra vegetables to bump up
the nutrient content and add colour.

INGREDIENTS

1 kg (2 lb 4 oz) rump steak, cut into strips
½ cup (75 g, 2¾ oz) plain (all-purpose) flour, to coat meat
olive oil, for frying
1 onion, thinly sliced
2 teaspoons crushed garlic
250 g (9 oz) mushrooms, sliced
½ red capsicum (pepper), deseeded and sliced
¼ cup (60 ml/2 fl oz) Worcestershire sauce
1½ cups (375 ml/13 fl oz) beef stock
1 tablespoon wholegrain mustard
1 handful of snow peas (mangetout)
½ cup (125 g/4½ oz) sour cream
pasta, rice, noodles or mashed potato, to serve

LET'S PUT IT ALL TOGETHER

1. Put the meat strips into a bowl with the flour and season with salt and pepper. Mix through to coat all the beef pieces in flour.
2. In a large non-stick frying pan over medium–high heat, put a splash of olive oil, then add the onion and garlic and cook until the onion softens.
3. Gradually add the meat to the pan and cook until it has browned.

4. Stir in the mushrooms and capsicum and cook until they soften.

5. Add the Worcestershire sauce, beef stock and mustard and stir through to combine. Reduce to a simmer and cook for 15 minutes.

7. Add the snow peas and sour cream. Stir through and cook for a further minute before removing from the heat.

8. Serve with pasta, rice, noodles or mashed potato.

SLOW COOKER MILD BEEF CURRY

SERVES 8

Whack the ingredients into your slow cooker and
you will be high-fiving yourself when you get home in
the evening to the best dinner you have had all week
(because you didn't stand over the stove cooking it).
Oh, and it tastes amazing too.

INGREDIENTS

1 tablespoon olive oil
1 onion, thinly sliced
1 tablespoon crushed garlic
1 kg (2 lb 4 oz) beef chuck steak, cut into cubes
4 potatoes, cut into cubes
1 carrot, chopped
1 celery stalk, thinly sliced
156 g Patak's Mild Butter Chicken Curry Paste, or mild curry paste
400 g (14 oz) tin diced tomatoes
200 ml (7 fl oz) light coconut milk

LET'S PUT IT ALL TOGETHER

1. If your slow cooker has a sauté function, as mine does, put
   a dash of oil, the onion, garlic and beef into the bowl and
   cook until the beef browns. Alternatively, do this step in a
   frying pan on the stove and then transfer the mixture to the
   slow cooker.

2. Add the remaining ingredients and stir to combine. Cover with the lid.
3. Set the slow cooker on low and cook for 8–10 hours depending on your slow cooker.
4. Serve with cooked rice or quinoa.

SLOW COOKER BEEF AND SWEET POTATO STEW

SERVES 6–8

This stew is easy to put together and the use
of sweet potato instead of regular potato adds
a lovely sweet flavour. It also has a lower GI and is
packed full of the nutrients we need as the
weather cools down.

INGREDIENTS

olive oil, for frying

1 onion, chopped

1 tablespoon crushed garlic

1 kg (2 lb 4 oz) beef chuck steak, cut into cubes

¼ cup (35 g/1¼ oz) plain (all-purpose) flour (you can swap for
  gluten-free flour)

½ teaspoon salt

½ teaspoon freshly ground black pepper

1 bay leaf

1 teaspoon sweet paprika

1 tablespoon Worcestershire sauce

1 cup (250 ml/9 fl oz) beef, chicken or vegetable stock

1 sweet potato, peeled and diced (about 2 cups)

2 carrots, chopped

cooked rice or pasta, to serve

LET'S PUT IT ALL TOGETHER

1. If your slow cooker has a sauté function, add a dash of olive oil, the onion and garlic and cook until softened and aromatic. Add the beef, then sprinkle with the flour, salt and pepper. Stir to coat and cook for 5 minutes or until the meat starts to brown. Alternatively, do this step in a frying pan, then transfer the beef mixture to the slow cooker.

2. Add the remaining ingredients, cover with the lid, set the slow cooker to low and cook for 8–10 hours or on high for 4 hours, depending on your slow cooker.

3. Serve with cooked rice or pasta.

SLOW-COOKED EYE ROUND ROAST WITH BALSAMIC GLAZE

SERVES 4–6

If you are looking for a melt-in-your-mouth beef roast then this is for you. The balsamic glaze is lovely and sweet and infuses the meat and vegetables with flavour.

INGREDIENTS

olive oil, for frying
1 onion, sliced
1 × 1 kg (2 lb 4 oz) beef eye round roast
1 cup (250 ml/9 fl oz) beef stock
½ cup (100 g/3½ oz) brown sugar
¼ cup (60 ml/2 fl oz) balsamic vinegar
1 tablespoon soy sauce (low sodium)
1 tablespoon crushed garlic
4 potatoes, quartered
2 carrots, cut into chunks
1 cup (140 g/5 oz) frozen peas
couscous, to serve (optional)

LET'S PUT IT ALL TOGETHER

1. Heat a frying pan on the stove or, if your slow cooker sautés, set it to that function. When hot, add a splash of oil, the onion and meat, brown the meat on all sides.
2. While it is browning, prepare the sauce.
3. In a bowl combine the stock, brown sugar, balsamic vinegar, soy sauce and garlic. Mix well to combine.

4. When the meat is brown, transfer it to the slow cooker or, if it's already in the slow cooker, set the slow cooker to slow cook function.

5. Add the vegetables and pour on the balsamic glaze, making sure the meat gets a good coating, and cover with the lid. Set to cook on low for 8 hours or high for 4 hours, depending on your slow cooker.

6. When the time is up, remove the liquid and put it in a small saucepan over medium heat. Simmer until the glaze reduces and thickens. Optional: leave half the liquid in the slow cooker and add I cup (190 g/6¾ oz) couscous while the slow cooker is still on. Leave in the slow cooker with the lid on for 10 minutes.

8. Slice the meat and serve with the vegetables and couscous, if you like, and top with the reduced balsamic glaze.

BEEF BRISKET POT ROAST

SERVES 4

You are one pot away from a deliciously succulent beef roast. Minimum effort, maximum taste and a great family meal. You can even make your own gravy with the juices in the pan.

INGREDIENTS

2 tablespoons olive oil
1 beef brisket pot roast, string left on
1 onion, chopped
2 garlic cloves, sliced
2 carrots, thickly sliced
4 potatoes, quartered
2 bay leaves
2 cups (500 ml/17 fl oz) beef stock or water
1 teaspoon dried or fresh thyme leaves
2 handfuls of green beans, topped and tailed
1 tablespoon cornflour (cornstarch), for gravy
crusty bread, to serve

LET'S PUT IT ALL TOGETHER

1. Preheat the oven to 160°C (315°F).
2. Put a flameproof casserole dish on the stove and heat the olive oil over high heat. Add the beef and brown on all sides. Season with salt and pepper as you turn.
3. Add the onion, garlic, carrot and potato, followed by the bay leaves, stock or water and thyme.

4. Bring to the boil, cover and transfer to the oven. Roast for 3 hours. You might like to turn the roast every hour, although I don't do this.

5. Remove the lid for the final 30 minutes of cooking and add the beans.

6. Remove from the oven and stand for 10 minutes before slicing the meat.

7. To make gravy from the juices, remove the meat and vegetables from the baking dish. Put the baking dish over medium–high heat on the stovetop and add the cornflour, dissolved in 2 tablespoons of water. Bring to a gentle boil, stirring constantly, until it starts to thicken.

8. Enjoy with crusty bread.

CLASSIC CHUNKY STEAK AND CHEESE PIE

SERVES 6–8

Pie night is always a favourite and homemade pies taste so much better than store-bought ones. Ready-made puff pastry makes this a quick dish to put together with plenty left over for another meal. I use rump steak so I don't have to cook the filling for hours. The filling can also be made the day before or frozen ready for a night when you are too busy to cook from scratch.

INGREDIENTS

olive oil, for frying

1 onion, chopped

2 tablespoons crushed garlic

500 g (1 lb 2 oz) rump steak, fat removed and diced

3 tablespoons cornflour (cornstarch)

2 cups (500 ml/17 fl oz) beef stock

1 teaspoon dried thyme

2 dried bay leaves

1 cup of chopped vegetables, such as carrots, peas or
    mushrooms (optional)

2 sheets of frozen puff pastry

cooking oil spray, for greasing

1 cup (100 g/3½ oz) grated tasty cheddar cheese

1 egg, whisked (155 g/5½ oz)

LET'S PUT IT ALL TOGETHER

1. Set a large saucepan on high heat on the stove. Add a splash of olive oil followed by the onion and garlic. Cook until the onion softens.

2. Add the steak and season with salt and pepper to taste, stirring until the meat is browned.

3. In a jug, combine the cornflour with the stock until dissolved. Pour into the saucepan and stir. Add the thyme and bay leaves and reduce to a simmer. (If using vegetables, add them now.) Cover with a lid and cook for 30 minutes. Check occasionally to make sure the meat isn't sticking to the bottom of the pan and give it a little stir.

4. After 30 minutes the meat should be nice and thick and resemble a pie filling consistency. Remove from the stove and allow to cool slightly. I like to place the saucepan into a sink filled with cold water and stir.

5. Preheat the oven to 200°C (400°F). Thaw the frozen puff pastry and spray the pie dish (25cm) with cooking oil so the pastry won't stick. Line the bottom of the dish with the pastry, covering the side and with a little overhanging. Spoon in the pie filling, top with the grated cheese and then finish with another sheet of puff pastry. Make sure you crimp the pastry together all around the edge to seal and prick the pastry with a fork to make vents.

6. Brush with the whisked egg and bake for 20 minutes or until the pastry is golden and puffed up. Allow to cool slightly before slicing and serving.

7. Enjoy with mashed potato and peas.

QUICK MONGOLIAN BEEF

SERVES 4–6

Don't reach for the takeaway (take-out) menu
to enjoy your favourite dish. This one is so easy to
make you will have it on the table in the same
amount of time it takes to place the order,
get into the car, pick up the meal and come
home again. Oh, and one pot means less dishes,
so it's a win–win situation.

INGREDIENTS

2 tablespoons olive oil
500 g (1 lb 2 oz) beef stir-fry strips
3 tablespoons cornflour (cornstarch)
1 tablespoon crushed garlic
1 tablespoon crushed fresh ginger
½ cup (125 ml/4 fl oz) soy sauce (low sodium)
½ cup (100 g/3½ oz) brown sugar
500 g (1 lb 2 oz) stir-fry vegetables, such as broccoli, carrots,
    snow peas (mangetout)
cooked rice, to serve

LET'S PUT IT ALL TOGETHER

1. Heat the olive oil in a large non-stick frying pan over high heat.
   While the oil is heating, dust the beef strips in the cornflour.
2. Put the garlic, ginger and beef with any leftover cornflour into
   the hot oil and cook until lightly browned.

3. Mix together the soy sauce and brown sugar with I cup (250 ml/9 fl oz) of water and pour it over the beef. Reduce to low heat and cook, stirring, for about 5 minutes or until the sauce thickens. Remove from the heat.
4. Steam the vegetables and serve with the cooked rice.

BARBECUE BEEF STEAK AND MUSHROOM SKEWERS

MAKES ABOUT 8 SKEWERS

I love barbecue season: it gets you cooking outside and saves your kitchen from the mess. These skewers are perfect to put together in the morning, ready to be cooked in the evening or for lunch. Add a crunchy side salad and bread and you're done.

INGREDIENTS

2 tablespoons crushed garlic

¼ cup (60 ml/2 fl oz) barbecue sauce (spicy ketchup)

3 tablespoons Worcestershire sauce

500 g (1 lb 2 oz) rump steak, trimmed and cut into 2-cm (¾-inch) cubes

15 button mushrooms, cut in half if large

2 zucchini (courgettes), sliced 1 cm (⅜ inch) thick

LET'S PUT IT ALL TOGETHER

1. Combine the garlic, barbecue sauce and Worcestershire sauce in a bowl and season with a sprinkling of salt and pepper. Add the steak and stir to coat. Leave in the fridge to marinate for a minimum of 30 minutes or throughout the day.

2. If using wooden skewers, soak them in water for at least 10 minutes to prevent them from burning during cooking. When ready to cook, simply assemble your skewers by threading on a piece of meat, a piece of mushroom and a slice of zucchini, repeating three times on each skewer.
3. Heat a barbecue or chargrill pan on high and cook the skewers until browned on all sides. Alternatively, you can put them into a 200°C (400°F) oven and bake for 25 minutes.

CHICKEN

Chicken is one of the most versatile and budget-friendly meats for a family. From chicken pieces to fillets to our favourite, roasting a whole chicken, you will never get bored with serving it for dinner.

LAYERED MEXICAN CHICKEN

SERVES 4–6

All your favourite Mexican flavours come together
in a one-pot dinner. Layer them up and then simply
scoop out to serve this flavour-packed meal.
Serve with extra corn chips for a fun way to eat.

INGREDIENTS

olive oil, for frying
3 large skinless chicken breast fillets, diced
1 cup (250 g/9 oz) mild tomato salsa
125 g (4½ oz) light cream cheese
425 g (15 oz) tin black beans, drained and rinsed
1 cup (245 g/8¾ oz) sour cream
200 g (7 oz) tin corn kernels
2 tomatoes, chopped
1 cup (50 g/1¾ oz) crushed corn chips
1 cup (125 g/4½ oz) grated mozzarella cheese
cooked rice and extra corn chips, to serve

LET'S PUT IT ALL TOGETHER

1. Preheat the oven to 180°C (350°F). Heat the olive oil in a
   large non-stick frying pan over high heat and add the diced
   chicken, cooking until lightly golden on all sides. Remove from
   the heat.

2. Add the salsa, cream cheese and black beans to the chicken and
   mix through.

3. Using a pie dish or similar ovenproof container, begin to layer: first the chicken mixture, then the sour cream, corn kernels, tomato, crushed corn chips and finally the mozzarella cheese. Bake for 25 minutes or until golden and bubbling.
4. Serve with cooked rice and extra corn chips.

ONE-PAN CHICKEN FAJITAS

SERVES 4–6

I love it when I can pop a meal into the oven and carry on with doing other things, such as wrangling bath time and homework. In this dish, once you get everything into the pan it will cook happily in the oven.

INGREDIENTS

3 skinless chicken breast fillets, cut into strips
1 onion, sliced
1 green capsicum (pepper), sliced
1 red capsicum (pepper), sliced
olive oil, for drizzling
3 tablespoons Taco Seasoning (see page 331)
8–12 tortillas
sour cream, to serve
lime and fresh coriander (cilantro) (optional)

LET'S PUT IT ALL TOGETHER

1. Preheat the oven to 180°C (350°F). Put the chicken and vegetables into a non-stick ovenproof dish. Drizzle with some olive oil and sprinkle on the taco seasoning.
2. Using your hands or a spoon, toss to coat the ingredients evenly with the oil and seasoning.
3. Bake for 30 minutes or until the chicken is golden and the vegetables have softened.
4. Spoon onto the tortillas and top with the sour cream and, if you like, a squeeze of lime and some coriander.

EASY CHICKEN ENCHILADAS

SERVES 6–12

This is a great dish to make with leftover
roast chicken or a store-bought roast chicken,
for an easy midweek meal that will have
everyone asking for more.

INGREDIENTS

olive oil, for frying
1 onion, chopped
4 cups (700 g/1 lb 9 oz) shredded cooked chicken
375 g (13 oz) enchilada sauce
1 cup (245 g/8¾ oz) sour cream
2 cups (250 g/9 oz) grated mozzarella cheese
12 tortillas

LET'S PUT IT ALL TOGETHER

1. Preheat the oven to 180°C (350°F). Heat a splash of olive oil in
   a large non-stick frying pan over high heat. Add the onion and
   cook until it softens. Reduce to medium heat, add the cooked
   chicken and stir to combine.
2. Pour in half of the enchilada sauce, followed by the sour cream,
   and stir to combine. Remove from the heat.
3. Divide the chicken mixture and half the mozzarella cheese
   evenly between the tortillas. Roll the tortillas around the filling
   and place in an ovenproof dish in a single layer.

4. Pour the remaining enchilada sauce over the enchiladas, then scatter with the remaining cheese.
5. Cover the dish with foil and bake for 25 minutes, removing the foil for the final 10 minutes of cooking time, to brown the cheese and tortillas.

CHICKEN TERIYAKI CASSEROLE

SERVES 6

This is kinda like a fried rice dish, except that everything is cooked together in the oven, thus giving it the title of casserole. It's a little more saucy than fried rice.

INGREDIENTS

olive oil, for frying

1 onion, chopped

1 tablespoon crushed garlic

4 boneless, skinless chicken thigh fillets, chopped

1½ cups (220 g/7¾ oz) medium grain rice

500 g (1 lb 2 oz) stir-fry vegetables, such as broccoli, carrots, snow peas (mangetout)

¾ cup (185 ml/6 fl oz) soy sauce (low sodium)

½ cup (100 g/3½ oz) brown sugar

1 teaspoon ground ginger

2 tablespoons cornflour (cornstarch)

LET'S PUT IT ALL TOGETHER

1. Preheat the oven to 180°C (350°F). Set a flameproof casserole dish over high heat. Add a splash of olive oil followed by the onion and garlic. Cook until the onion softens and then add the chicken. Cook until the chicken is lightly browned. Remove from the heat.

2. Add the rice and stir-fry vegetables and stir through to combine.
3. In a bowl or jug, mix the soy sauce, brown sugar, ground ginger and cornflour with 3 cups (750 ml/26 fl oz) of water. Make sure the cornflour dissolves completely. Pour over the chicken mixture and stir through.
4. Place the lid on the casserole dish and bake for 30 minutes. Check halfway through the cooking time and give it a gentle stir to make sure the rice isn't sticking. It is ready to eat when the rice is cooked.

CREAMY MUSHROOM CHICKEN

SERVES 6–8

This delicious family casserole is filled with great flavours; ones that everyone will enjoy. It uses one pan and one baking dish, helping to keep the dishwashing down (and keeping us happy).

INGREDIENTS

olive oil, for frying

7 chicken 'lovely legs' (see note)

1 onion, thinly sliced

10 mushrooms, thinly sliced

1 tablespoon crushed garlic

3 tablespoons butter

3 tablespoons plain (all-purpose) flour

1½ cups (375 ml/13 fl oz) chicken stock

400 ml (14 fl oz) tin Carnation Light & Creamy Evaporated Milk, or other evaporated milk

juice of ½ lemon

pasta, rice or mashed potato, to serve

LET'S PUT IT ALL TOGETHER

1. Preheat the oven to 160°C (315°F).
2. In a frying pan over high heat, heat a little olive oil and then add the chicken. Cook to brown on all sides, then remove from the frying pan and transfer to a baking dish.

3. Put the onion, mushrooms and garlic into the same frying pan you cooked the chicken in and cook until they are lightly golden and softened a little. Remove from the pan and scatter over the cooked chicken.
4. In the same frying pan, melt the butter. Add the flour and stir through for 1 minute. Slowly add the chicken stock, whisking after each addition. Follow this by adding the evaporated milk, whisking after each addition. Season with salt and pepper and the lemon juice. Pour the sauce over the chicken and mushroom mixture.
5. Cover the baking dish with foil and bake for 90 minutes.
6. Serve with pasta, rice or mashed potato.

TIP The sauce may split depending on the amount of skin on the chicken you use. Simply remix before serving.

NOTE 'Lovely legs' are chicken drumsticks with the skin and lower part of the bone removed. If you can't find them, use skinless chicken breast fillets cut into strips instead and bake for 45 minutes or until the chicken is cooked through.

ONE-PAN ORANGE CHICKEN

SERVES 4–6

This dish is tangy, sweet and fresh. I have added frozen peas, but it is versatile enough that you could use other small-cut frozen vegetables like corn, carrots or beans. Work with what your family loves and you can't go wrong with the lovely orange sauce.

INGREDIENTS

olive oil, for frying

1.5 kg (3 lb 5 oz) chicken pieces (I cut up a whole chicken into 10 segments)

plain (all-purpose) flour, for dusting

3 teaspoons crushed garlic

finely grated zest of 1 orange

juice of 2 oranges

⅓ cup (115 g/4 oz) honey

⅓ cup (80 ml/3 fl oz) soy sauce (low sodium)

¼ cup (60 ml/2 fl oz) rice wine vinegar (optional)

½ teaspoon ground ginger

½ teaspoon freshly ground black pepper

3 tablespoons cornflour (cornstarch)

1–2 cups (140–280 g/5–10 oz) frozen peas or other vegetables of choice

cooked quinoa, or rice, to serve

LET'S PUT IT ALL TOGETHER

1. Heat a drizzle of olive oil in a large frying pan over high heat.
2. Dust the chicken pieces with the flour, shaking off any excess.

3. Put the chicken pieces into the hot pan. Cook on the first side for 5 minutes, then turn and cook for a further 3 minutes on the other side until it is nice and golden on both sides.
4. Meanwhile, combine the garlic, orange zest and juice, honey, soy sauce, rice wine vinegar (if using), ginger, pepper and cornflour in a jug. Whisk until all of the ingredients are well combined.
5. When the chicken is cooked, turn the heat down to medium. Pour the orange sauce over the chicken pieces and turn to coat. Cook until the sauce thickens, then cover the pan and cook on medium–low heat for 10 minutes.
6. Add the frozen vegetables and cook for a further 10 minutes.
7. Serve with quinoa or rice.

BAKED SAUCY LEMON CHICKEN BREASTS

SERVES 4–6

This is such a simple way to turn chicken breasts into a low-fat delicious meal. Full of lemon zing, but balanced with honey, so your family will love the flavours. Serve with steamed vegetables and rice for a complete meal.

INGREDIENTS

1 tablespoon lemon zest
juice of 2 lemons
2 tablespoons honey
4 small skinless chicken breast fillets (or 2 large, sliced lengthways)
finey chopped fresh flat-leaf (Italian) parsley, to serve
cooked rice and steamed vegetables, to serve

LET'S PUT IT ALL TOGETHER

1. Preheat the oven to 180°C (350°F).
2. In a jug, combine the lemon zest and juice, honey and a sprinkling of salt and pepper. Put the chicken breasts into a baking dish and pour the sauce over them. Coat all sides of the chicken well. Cover the baking dish with a lid or foil and bake for 20 minutes.
3. Remove the lid or foil from the baking dish and turn the oven up to 200°C (400°F). Cook for a further 5–10 minutes until the chicken starts to turn golden on top.

4. Remove from the oven and scatter with the parsley.
5. Serve with rice and steamed vegetables. Pour any leftover sauce in the baking dish over the chicken once it is on the plate.

ONE-PAN MANGO CHICKEN

SERVES 4–6

Light and tasty, this dish will become a family favourite
in no time. Its sweet flavour will appeal to the younger
family members and, being low in fat, it makes
an ideal weeknight meal.

INGREDIENTS

800 g (1 lb 12 oz) tin mango cheeks in natural juice, drained and
   juice reserved
4 skinless chicken breast fillets
1 onion, sliced
1 red capsicum (pepper), sliced
410 g (14 oz) tin baby corn spears, drained and rinsed
2 chicken stock cubes
steamed rice, to serve

LET'S PUT IT ALL TOGETHER

1. Preheat the oven to 200°C (400°F).
2. Put 4 mango cheeks into a food processor or blender and
    process until smooth.
3. Lay the chicken breasts in an ovenproof dish. Cover with the
    mango purée, followed by the onion, red capsicum and baby
    corn spears.
4. Crumble the chicken stock cubes into the mango juice, season
    with salt and pepper and stir through. Pour this over the chicken
    and vegetables and toss to coat well. Cover the dish with a lid
    or foil.

5. Bake for 25–30 minutes until the chicken bounces back when touched.
6. Cut the remaining mango cheeks into cubes and add to the dish just before serving.
7. Serve with steamed rice.

CHICKEN FILO PILLOWS

MAKES 4

....

Wrap up an endless combination of fillings in low-fat filo pastry. I am using our family's favourite combination of chicken breast, camembert, baby spinach and wholegrain mustard. Prep in the morning and leave in the fridge until dinnertime: too easy.

....

INGREDIENTS

12 sheets of filo pastry
cooking oil spray
2 skinless chicken breast fillets, sliced in half lengthways
100 g (3½ oz) camembert cheese, sliced
150 g baby spinach leaves
1 tablespoon wholegrain mustard

LET'S PUT IT ALL TOGETHER

1. Preheat the oven to 180°C (350°F). Line a baking tray with baking paper and set aside. Lay one sheet of filo pastry on the work surface and spray it with cooking oil, then add another two sheets in the same manner.
2. Lay half a chicken breast in the middle of the short end, leaving a 5-cm (2-inch) space at the top. Add a quarter of the camembert and baby spinach, then spread 1 teaspoon of mustard on the pastry beside the chicken breast and season with salt and pepper.

3. Fold and roll the pillow: fold the top of the pastry over the filling, then fold the two long edges into the centre. Spray with cooking oil and roll until the filling is completely enclosed and finish with another spray of cooking oil. Place onto the prepared baking tray and repeat to make another three pillows. Bake for 30 minutes.

4. Serve with a side salad or some risotto.

BAKED PESTO CHICKEN WITH PASTA SAUCE

SERVES 4–5

I'm all about quick one-pan dinners, especially after a busy day or if I am late home from work. This is another great dinner that the whole family can enjoy. The pesto and pasta sauce give this dish its flavour, which means you don't have to worry about seasonings, herbs and spices as it's already done. You literally throw this together and walk away: my kinda dinner.

INGREDIENTS

500 g (1 lb 2 oz) boneless, skinless chicken thigh fillets
95 g (3¼ oz) basil pesto
1 zucchini (courgette), thinly sliced lengthways
400 g (14 oz) ready-made pasta sauce, such as napolitana
1 cup (100 g/3½ oz) grated cheddar or mozzarella cheese
pasta or ravioli, to serve

LET'S PUT IT ALL TOGETHER

1. Preheat the oven to 180°C (350°F). Put the chicken thighs in a baking dish and rub the pesto into the chicken. Lay the chicken out flat once coated. Lay the zucchini strips on top of the pesto chicken.
2. Pour on the pasta sauce and scatter with the cheese. Cover with a lid or foil and bake for 35 minutes.

3. Check that the chicken is cooked by making sure it is firm when pushed with your finger. If it is still soft, return it to the oven for a further 5–10 minutes.
4. Serve with pasta or cheese ravioli.

TIP The type of basil pesto and pasta sauce will determine the flavour of this dish, so use ones that are already family favourites. I use Aldi Basil Pesto and Aldi Organic Pasta Sauce.

NOTE You can swap the zucchini for eggplant (aubergine) or capsicum (pepper).

CHICKEN AND PRAWN PAELLA

SERVES 4–6

Paella means pan and you will only need one to create this delicious dinner. It's simple enough to cook on a weeknight and special enough to be cooked for family and friends.

INGREDIENTS

2 cups (500 ml/17 fl oz) chicken stock
a pinch of saffron threads (optional)
olive oil, for frying
4 boneless, skinless chicken thigh fillets, cut into cubes
200 g (7 oz) small raw prawns (shrimp), peeled and deveined, tail intact
1 onion, chopped
1 red capsicum (pepper), chopped
1 large tomato, chopped
2 tablespoons sweet paprika
1 cup (220 g/ 7¾ oz) medium-grain rice
½ cup (75 g/2¾ oz) frozen peas
1 spring onion (scallion), thinly sliced, to garnish

LET'S PUT IT ALL TOGETHER

1. Bring the chicken stock to the boil in a small saucepan and add the saffron threads (if using). Set aside.
2. Heat some olive oil in a large frying pan or an electric wok. Add the chicken and prawns and cook for 3 minutes or until golden brown. Remove from the pan.

3. Add the onion and capsicum to the pan and cook for 2 minutes or until soft. Add the tomato and paprika and stir to combine. Return the chicken and prawns to the mixture, then scatter the rice over the mix.
4. Pour in the hot stock and reduce the heat to low. Cook for 15 minutes or until most of the moisture has been absorbed by the rice. Add the peas and cover with a lid, cooking for a further 5 minutes.
5. Scatter the spring onion over the top and enjoy.

TIP If fresh prawns are hard to come by, swap for frozen prawns.

HOMEMADE APRICOT CHICKEN

SERVES 4–6

....

I don't like to use a lot of ready-made meal bases because they are expensive and you really don't know what you are eating. They seem like a quick option but making them from scratch doesn't actually require that much more work.

....

INGREDIENTS

2 large (800 g/1 lb 12 oz) tins apricot halves in syrup
olive oil, for frying
1 tablespoon crushed garlic
1 onion, chopped
6 boneless, skinless chicken thigh fillets, diced
2 carrots, chopped
1 tablespoon chicken stock powder
1 teaspoon garam masala
cooked rice, to serve

LET'S PUT IT ALL TOGETHER

1. Preheat the oven to 180°C (350°F).
2. Put one tin of apricot halves, including the syrup, into a food processor or blender and process until smooth.
3. Heat a flameproof casserole dish on the stovetop on medium–high heat. Add a splash of olive oil, then the garlic and onion and cook, stirring occasionally, until the onion softens.
4. Add the chicken and cook for 5 minutes until golden. Add the carrot and stir through.

5. Mix the apricot purée with I cup (250 ml/9 fl oz) of water, the chicken stock powder and garam masala and pour into the casserole dish. Reduce to a simmer.

6. Transfer to the oven and cook for 25 minutes.

7. Drain the other tin of apricot halves and add half (the other half can be placed in an airtight container and stored in the fridge to use in baking) to the casserole. Taste to see if you need to add any salt and pepper, stir through and return the dish to the oven for another 5 minutes.

8. Serve with rice.

SLOW COOKER HONEY MUSTARD CHICKEN

SERVES 4–6

Making the honey mustard flavour at home is so simple.
No need to worry about packet mixes or jars of honey
mustard: this recipe uses basic pantry items to give you
the same, if not even better, flavour that the whole
family will love. Both of my boys devour this meal,
so it definitely passes the kid test.

INGREDIENTS

olive oil, for frying
2 spring onions (scallions), white part only, thinly sliced
1 teaspoon crushed garlic
6 boneless, skinless chicken thigh fillets or 3–4 skinless chicken
    breast fillets
⅓ cup (115 g/4 oz) honey
⅓ cup (90 g/3¼ oz) wholegrain mustard
3 tablespoons hot water
1 teaspoon chicken stock powder
2 carrots, sliced
1 cup (200 g/7 oz) corn kernels (fresh, tinned or frozen)
⅓ cup (80 ml/2½ fl oz) thickened (whipping) cream
mashed potato, rice or pasta, to serve

LET'S PUT IT ALL TOGETHER

1. If your slow cooker has a sauté setting, put a splash of olive oil, the spring onion, garlic and chicken into it and brown the chicken on all sides. If your slow cooker doesn't sauté, do this in a frying pan, then transfer to the slow cooker.

2. Combine the honey, mustard, hot water and chicken stock powder in a bowl. Pour this over the browned chicken in the slow cooker. Add the carrot and mix everything together. Cover with the lid. Set to low for 6–8 hours.

3. Add the corn kernels and cream to the slow cooker and stir to combine.

4. Serve with mashed potato, rice or pasta.

CASSEROLE DISH VERSION Brown the chicken in a flameproof casserole dish on the stovetop, then cook covered in a low heat oven (160°C/315°F) for 3 hours. Alternatively, simmer on the stovetop for 3–4 hours, turning the chicken every hour or so.

ONE-PAN CREAMY CHICKEN, EGGPLANT AND TOMATO

SERVES 4–6

What I love about eggplant (aubergine) is that once you peel the skin off, its texture is almost undetectable. This is a great meal to serve with pasta knowing that you have added some extra vegetables into your family's diet.

INGREDIENTS

olive oil, for frying

1 onion, chopped

1 tablespoon crushed garlic

2 skinless chicken breast fillets, diced

1 eggplant (aubergine), peeled and chopped

4 large tomatoes, chopped

1 cup (250 ml/9 fl oz) chicken stock

2 tablespoons sugar

2 tablespoons sour cream

pasta, to serve

LET'S PUT IT ALL TOGETHER

1. Heat a large non-stick frying pan over medium–high heat. Add a splash of olive oil, followed by the onion and garlic. Cook until the onion softens.

2. Add the chicken and cook until golden. Add the eggplant and cook, stirring, for 5 minutes.

3. Add in the tomato, chicken stock, sugar and a sprinkling of salt and pepper and stir through. Reduce to a simmer and cook for 10 minutes, stirring regularly.
4. Remove from the heat and stir the sour cream through.
5. Serve with pasta.

OTHER MEATS

Ham, bacon, pork and lamb are perfect in pastas,
risottos and stews, just to name a few.
I always have ham in the fridge and use it to complete
a meal when the fridge is running low before
grocery shopping day.

ONE-PAN PESTO AND HAM GNOCCHI CASSEROLE

SERVES 4

My weeknight saviours are one-pan dinners.
They are so quick and easy to prepare and the best part
is fewer dishes to wash. This one-pan gnocchi casserole
is a winner of a family dinner, filled with ham,
cheese and, of course, potato gnocchi. You just know
everyone will be happy eating it.

INGREDIENTS

1 tablespoon olive oil
1 onion, chopped
500 g (1 lb 2 oz) potato gnocchi
¼ cup (60 g/2¼ oz) sundried tomato pesto
250 g (9 oz) sliced ham, chopped
½ cup (125 ml/9 fl oz) chicken stock
2 handfuls of baby spinach leaves (optional)
½ cup (125 ml/4 fl oz) Carnation Lite Cooking Cream, or other
    light cooking cream
½ cup (65 g/2½ oz) grated mozzarella cheese

LET'S PUT IT ALL TOGETHER

1. Heat the olive oil in a large non-stick ovenproof frying pan over
   medium–high heat. Add the onion and cook until it softens.

2. Reduce to low heat and add the gnocchi and sundried tomato pesto, stir to combine, and cook for 1 minute. Add the ham and chicken stock and reduce to a simmer. Cook for 5 minutes or until the gnocchi starts to soften. Stir in the spinach (if using).
3. Pour in the cooking cream and cook for a further 5 minutes. Remove from the heat and sprinkle on the cheese. Place the pan under the grill (broiler) and cook until the cheese melts and becomes lightly golden.

NO-STIR BACON AND MUSHROOM RISOTTO

SERVES 4–6

Risotto doesn't have to be time-consuming. A risotto
can actually fend for itself and cook quite sufficiently
without all the mixing. The secret to this is a heavy-based
saucepan or flameproof casserole dish with a lid,
to prevent the rice from sticking.
This risotto will cook happily on the stovetop
or in the oven, giving you hands-free time to get
baths done, homework sorted or just catch up
on things before dinner.

INGREDIENTS

olive oil, for frying
1 onion, finely chopped
2 garlic cloves, thinly sliced
10 button mushrooms, cut into sixths
1 celery stalk, finely chopped
200 g (7 oz) rindless streaky bacon (I use D'Orsogna), chopped
1 cup (220 g/7¾ oz) arborio rice
¼ head of cauliflower, chopped (optional)
5 cups (1.25 litres/44 fl oz) vegetable stock
25 g (1 oz) butter
½ cup (45 g/1½ oz) grated parmesan cheese

LET'S PUT IT ALL TOGETHER

1. Heat a heavy-based saucepan or flameproof casserole dish on medium–high. Add a drizzle of olive oil followed by the onion, garlic, mushrooms, celery and bacon. Cook until the vegetables start to soften.
2. Add the rice and mix to coat the grains well.
3. Add the cauliflower (if using), the stock and butter to the pan. You can either leave it cooking on medium–low heat on the stovetop or transfer it to the oven, preheated to 180°C (350°F). Cover with the lid and cook for 30 minutes until all the liquid is absorbed by the rice.
4. Add the parmesan cheese, season with salt and pepper and mix well.

SATAY PORK STIR-FRY

SERVES 4

....

This recipe is very versatile. You can change up
the vegetables to suit what your family likes or
what you have in the fridge. Frozen vegetables
are also suitable.

....

INGREDIENTS

1 packet (450 g/16 oz) fresh hokkein noodles
olive oil, for frying
½ onion, thinly sliced
2 garlic cloves, thinly sliced
250 g (9 oz) pork fillet, thinly sliced
1 red capsicum (pepper), sliced
½ head of broccoli, cut into florets
1 zucchini (courgette), cut into batons
1 carrot, thinly sliced
3 tablespoons peanut butter
2 cups (500 ml/17 fl oz) chicken stock

LET'S PUT IT ALL TOGETHER

1. Prepare the noodles according to the instructions on the packet.
   Most suggest soaking in boiling water for 10 minutes.
2. Heat some olive oil in a wok or large frying pan over high heat.
   Add the onion and garlic and cook until they soften. Add the
   pork and cook, stirring regularly, until lightly browned. Remove
   from the pan.

3. Put the vegetables into the pan and cook for 1 minute. Add the peanut butter and stock and mix well. Simmer for 5 minutes to let the sauce reduce and thicken.
4. Return the cooked pork mixture to the wok, then add the drained noodles. Stir well and serve immediately.

MOROCCAN LAMB AND SWEET POTATO STEW

SERVES 4–6

Nothing makes you feel more warm and cosy than a delicious aromatic stew. This one is slightly sweet and packed full of flavour. Perfect served with rice.

INGREDIENTS

1 kg (2 lb 4 oz) lamb shoulder, trimmed and diced
2 tablespoons Moroccan seasoning
2 tablespoons olive oil
1 onion, chopped
2 tablespoons crushed garlic
2 tablespoons tomato paste
1 large sweet potato, peeled and chopped
1½ cups (375 ml/13 fl oz) chicken stock
cooked rice, to serve

LET'S PUT IT ALL TOGETHER

1. Preheat the oven to 160°C (315°F).
2. Put the lamb in a bowl and sprinkle on the seasoning. Toss to coat the lamb well. Set aside.
3. Heat the olive oil in a flameproof casserole dish over medium–high heat and add the onion and garlic. Cook, stirring, until the onion softens. Add the coated lamb and cook until the meat has browned.

4. Stir through the tomato paste and sweet potato and cook for
    1 minute. Reduce to a simmer and pour in the stock. Cover with
    the lid and transfer to the oven, cooking for 2 hours.
5. Serve with rice.

SLOW COOKED LAMB FOREQUARTER CHOPS

SERVES 4

Turn the humble lamb chop into the most delicious slow-cooked lamb meal. Full of vegetables, tomato-infused juices and melt-in-the-mouth lamb, this dish is so easy to make, you'll be making it regularly in winter.

INGREDIENTS

6 lamb forequarter chops
olive oil, for sprinkling
½ butternut pumpkin (squash), peeled and cubed
2 carrots, chopped into 2-cm (¾-inch) pieces
6 mushrooms, sliced
1 onion, sliced
2 teaspoons crushed garlic
410 g (14 oz) tin tomato purée
chicken stock (enough to fill the empty tomato tin)
1 tablespoon fresh rosemary leaves (or use 1 teaspoon dried)
feta cheese, crumbled, to serve
chopped spring onions (scallions), to serve

LET'S PUT IT ALL TOGETHER

1. Preheat the oven to 150°C (300°F).
2. Sprinkle the lamb chops with salt and pepper and drizzle on a little olive oil. Put them into a hot frying pan and cook for about 5 minutes on each side until browned and the fat has started to render.

3. Meanwhile, put the pumpkin, carrot, half the mushrooms, half the onion and the garlic into a baking dish. When the chops have finished browning, place them on top of the vegetables in the dish.
4. Pour the tomato purée and then the chicken stock over the chops. Top with the remaining mushrooms and onion. Sprinkle with the rosemary.
5. Bake for 3 hours.
6. Scatter with the feta cheese and spring onions to serve.
7. Enjoy with some crusty bread.

MARINATED LAMB LOIN CHOPS

SERVES 4–6

Garlic and rosemary love lamb and this simple marinade
will make your lamb chops taste amazing with not very
much effort. Perfect for barbecue season.

INGREDIENTS

1 tablespoon chopped fresh rosemary

2 tablespoons dijon mustard

2 tablespoons crushed garlic

2 tablespoons olive oil

1 kg (2 lb 4 oz) lamb loin chops

potato salad or garden salad, to serve

LET'S PUT IT ALL TOGETHER

1. Combine the rosemary, mustard, garlic, olive oil and a sprinkling
   of salt and pepper in a large bowl. Mix well.
2. Add the lamb chops and toss to coat. Transfer to the fridge
   until you are ready to cook them. They need to marinate for a
   minimum of 30 minutes.
3. Heat a barbecue or chargrill pan on high heat and cook the lamb
   for 10 minutes on the first side, then flip and cook for another
   5 minutes, making sure the chops are cooked through.
4. Serve with potato salad or garden salad.

SEAFOOD

Seafood can sometimes be tricky to include in our diets,
especially with the younger members of the family.
These are some great ways to boost your family's intake.

PRAWN LINGUINE

SERVES 6–8

The prawns are the star of this meal and rightfully so:
they cook quickly, taste great and will keep everyone
happy. This is an ideal quick midweek dinner.

INGREDIENTS

500 g (1 lb 2 oz) linguine
50 g (1¾ oz) butter
2 tablespoons crushed garlic
1 kg (2 lb 4 oz) raw prawns (shrimp), peeled and deveined (you
    can use frozen prawns if you like)
1 cup (250 ml/9 fl oz) light cooking cream
1 cup (100 g/3½ oz) grated parmesan cheese
finely chopped fresh flat-leaf (Italian) parsley, to serve

LET'S PUT IT ALL TOGETHER

1. Cook the linguine according to the instructions on the packet.
2. Meanwhile, heat a large non-stick frying pan over medium–high heat.
3. Melt the butter, then add the garlic and prawns, cooking until the
   prawns turn pink.
4. Reduce to low heat and pour in the cream, season with salt and
   pepper and cook for 2 minutes. Remove from the heat.
5. Drain the cooked linguine, add half the parmesan to the prawns
   and sauce and toss through the pasta.
6. Serve with the remaining parmesan cheese and scatter with the
   parsley.

TUNA AND VEGETABLE PASTA BAKE

SERVES 4–6

When the boys were littler I used to cook this dish with dinosaur-shaped pasta and they would demolish everything on their plates. Now we cook it with shell pasta for a completely family-friendly meal.

INGREDIENTS

200 g (7 oz) shell pasta
25 g (1 oz) butter
1 tablespoon plain (all-purpose) flour
2 cups (500 ml/17 fl oz) milk
1 cup (100 g/3½ oz) grated tasty cheddar cheese
2 cups (290 g/10¼ oz) frozen pea, corn and carrot mixture, thawed
185 g (6½ oz) tin tuna chunks in springwater, drained
½ cup (55 g/2 oz) dry breadcrumbs

LET'S PUT IT ALL TOGETHER

1. Preheat the oven to 180°C (350°F).
2. Cook the pasta, following the packet instructions. Meanwhile, melt the butter in a saucepan, then add the flour and cook, stirring constantly, for about 2 minutes.
3. Gradually add the milk, stirring constantly with a whisk, to the flour mixture. When it begins to thicken, add the cheese and continue stirring for a further minute. Remove from the heat.

4. Add the vegetable mixture and tuna to the white sauce, season with salt and pepper and stir through. Drain the pasta and add it to the sauce mix, stirring to combine.

5. Pour the mixture into a baking dish and sprinkle on the breadcrumbs.

6. Bake for 15 minutes until the breadcrumbs are toasted and golden.

SMOKED SALMON AND ZUCCHINI FETTUCCINE

SERVES 4–6

This is such a flavour-packed quick-and-easy dinner.
In the time it takes to cook the pasta, the sauce
will be cooked as well.

INGREDIENTS

250 g (9 oz) fettuccine

1 tablespoon olive oil

1 onion, chopped

1 tablespoon crushed garlic

1 zucchini (courgette), chopped

1 cup (250 ml/9 fl oz) Carnation Lite Cooking Cream, or other
light cooking cream

½ cup (45 g/1 ½ oz) grated parmesan cheese (optional)

200 g (7 oz) smoked salmon

LET'S PUT IT ALL TOGETHER

1. Cook the pasta following the packet instructions.
2. Meanwhile, heat the olive oil in a large non-stick frying pan over medium–high heat and add the onion, garlic and zucchini. Cook, stirring occasionally, until the onion softens.
3. Reduce to low heat and pour in the cooking cream. Stir in the parmesan (if using), season with salt and pepper and break pieces of the smoked salmon into the sauce. Stir through and allow to simmer for 5 minutes. Remove from the heat.

4. Drain the cooked pasta and divide between serving plates. Spoon the smoked salmon and zucchini sauce over the pasta.

VEGETARIAN

These vegetarian dishes are a tasty and easy way to boost your family's vegetable intake or to add to your collection of meat-free meals.

ASPARAGUS AND CHEESE TART

SERVES 2–4

This couldn't be any easier to make. A couple of basic steps and you will have a quick dinner or lunch.

INGREDIENTS

1 sheet of frozen puff pastry, thawed
6 asparagus spears (if using tinned, drain well)
½ onion, thinly sliced
½ cup (65 g/2½ oz) grated mozzarella cheese (or use cheddar)

LET'S PUT IT ALL TOGETHER

1. Preheat the oven to 200°C (400°F).
2. Line a baking tray with baking paper. Lay the puff pastry sheet on the tray and fold up the edges about 1 cm (⅜ inch).
3. Lay the asparagus over the puff pastry, scatter the onion over the top, season with salt and pepper and top with the cheese.
4. Bake for 15 minutes or until the pastry is puffed up and golden and the cheese has melted.
5. Cut into squares to serve.

TIP Best enjoyed on the day of making.

ONE-PAN GREEN BEANS, CHICKPEAS AND NUTS

SERVES 4–8

Green beans—love them or hate them—can be
turned into a great vegetable-based meal or side dish.
I like to serve this dish with our Sunday roast.

INGREDIENTS

olive oil, for frying

500 g (1 lb 2 oz) green beans, topped and tailed

400 g (14 oz) tin chickpeas, drained and rinsed

3 tablespoons pine nuts

3 tablespoons crushed peanuts

juice of 1 lemon

LET'S PUT IT ALL TOGETHER

1. Heat a large non-stick frying pan over medium–high heat. Add a splash of olive oil and the green beans. Cook, stirring regularly, for 5 minutes.
2. Add the remaining ingredients and cook for a further 5 minutes, stirring.
3. Enjoy on its own, or serve as a side dish.

COUSCOUS-STUFFED CAPSICUMS

SERVES 4

Couscous and vegetable stuffed capsicums are deliciously easy. They are a sneaky way to get the family eating vegetables, as they are a little bit of fun.

INGREDIENTS

1½ cups (375 ml / 13 fl oz) boiling water
1 teaspoon vegetable stock powder
1 cup (190 g / 6¾ oz) couscous
1 tablespoon olive oil
1 onion, chopped
1 tablespoon crushed garlic
1 zucchini (courgette), chopped
½ cup (100 g / 3½ oz) corn kernels
4 red capsicums (peppers)
1 cup (125 g / 4½ oz) grated mozzarella cheese

LET'S PUT IT ALL TOGETHER

1. Preheat the oven to 180°C (350°F). Line a baking tray with baking paper.
2. Combine the boiling water and stock powder in a jug. Put the couscous into a bowl and pour the hot vegetable stock mixture over it. Cover the bowl with plastic wrap and set aside.

3. Heat a non-stick frying pan over medium–high heat. Add the olive oil, onion and garlic and cook until the onion softens. Add the zucchini and corn and cook for 5 minutes. Remove from the stove.

4. Use a fork to fluff up the couscous, then add the cooked vegetables and stir through.

5. Prepare the capsicums by slicing off the top and scooping out the seeds. Place on the prepared baking tray and spoon the couscous mixture into each capsicum. Top with the grated cheese. Bake for 20 minutes or until the cheese is melted and golden brown.

TIP If the capsicums (peppers) are large, cut in half widthways.

VEGETABLE AND COTTAGE CHEESE ROLLS

SERVES 6–8

These are a vegetarian-friendly take on a standard sausage roll. Filled with vegetables and cottage cheese, they make a light alternative that is perfect for any time of the day.

INGREDIENTS

1 cup (265 g/9¼ oz) cottage cheese
3 eggs, whisked
1 onion, grated
1 carrot, grated
1 zucchini (courgette), grated and excess liquid squeezed out
½ cup (100 g/3½ oz) corn kernels
1 cup (105 g/3⅝ oz) instant oats
½ cup (55 g/2 oz) dry breadcrumbs
3–4 sheets of frozen puff pastry, thawed
sesame seeds, for sprinkling

LET'S PUT IT ALL TOGETHER

1. Preheat the oven to 200°C (400°F). Line a baking tray with baking paper and set aside.
2. Combine all of the ingredients except the puff pastry and sesame seeds in a bowl (reserve a little of the egg to brush on top of the puff pastry) and mix well. You will probably need to get your hands into the mix to work it through well. Alternatively, you can put the ingredients into a food processor fitted with the plastic mixing blade and process gently to combine.

3. Cut the puff pastry sheets in half. Lay some of the filling along the middle of both halves and then wrap the pastry around the filling to form a sealed roll. With the sealed side down, slice into rolls of the desired length. Place them on the prepared baking tray. Repeat until all of the filling and pastry is used.

4. Brush the tops of the rolls with the reserved egg and sprinkle with the sesame seeds. Bake for 15 minutes or until the pastry is puffed up and golden.

5. Serve with your favourite dipping sauce (I like sweet chilli sauce with mine) and a side salad to make it a meal.

sweet treats

Whether you are simply satisfying a sweet tooth, or making an impressive dessert for family and friends, these recipes will soon become your favourites too.

FIVE-MINUTE MICROWAVE CARAMEL SAUCE

MAKES 10

What's the next best thing to chocolate sauce? Caramel sauce, of course. And what's better than caramel sauce? Five-minute microwave sauce made from common pantry and fridge items. Enjoy served warm over ice cream, spooned into tart cases or, dare I say it, eaten straight from the jar. Whichever way you eat it, you will want to make this recipe over and over again.

INGREDIENTS

2 egg yolks
20 g (¾ oz) butter
½ cup (125 ml/4 fl oz) milk
½ cup (110 g /3¾ oz) firmly packed brown sugar
1 tablespoon plain (all-purpose) flour (use gluten-free flour if you like)
1 teaspoon natural vanilla essence

LET'S PUT IT ALL TOGETHER

1. Put all of the ingredients in a microwave-safe bowl or container and give them a good whisk.
2. Put the bowl into the microwave and set to medium power. Cook for 5 minutes, making sure to stir after each minute. You know it's ready when it is thick and there are no lumps.
3. Store in an airtight container in the fridge. You can microwave individual amounts for about 10 seconds just before serving, if you want to eat it warm.

NO-HEAT CHOCOLATE MOUSSE

SERVES 6+

This is the quickest way to make chocolate mousse.
No heating required and only basic ingredients means
that it is a cheap dessert. Spoon into fancy little cups and
top with berries if you feel like being fancy.

INGREDIENTS

600 ml (21 fl oz) thickened (whipping) cream
1 tablespoon icing (confectioners') sugar
40 g (1 ½ oz) unsweetened cocoa powder
1 teaspoon peppermint essence (optional)
choc chips, for decoration
berries, to serve

LET'S PUT IT ALL TOGETHER

1. You will need a standing electric mixer fitted with the whisk attachment or a handheld electric beater. Put the cream, sugar and cocoa (and peppermint essence, if using) into a bowl. Whisk until the cream thickens and soft peaks hold.
2. Spoon into individual serving cups or one large bowl. Sprinkle the chocolate chips on top and put in the fridge for 30 minutes or until you are ready to eat.
3. Before serving, add the berries.

MUM'S PAVLOVA

SERVES 6–8

When it comes to pavlovas, in our family my mum
is the master: I don't even try to make them as no
one does it better than her. Mum's pavlova has a
lovely crunchy outside and a soft fluffy inside,
topped with fresh cream and fruit.

INGREDIENTS

5 large egg whites
¾ cup (165 g/5¾ oz) caster (super fine) sugar
1 teaspoon natural vanilla essence
1 teaspoon white vinegar
1 tablespoon cornflour (cornstarch)
whipped cream and fruit, to serve

LET'S PUT IT ALL TOGETHER

1. Preheat the oven to 150°C (300°F). Line a baking tray with
   baking paper and set aside.
2. Beat the egg whites using a stand electric mixer fitted with the
   whisk attachment with a pinch of salt until very stiff peaks form,
   then add half the sugar, one spoonful at a time, beating well after
   each addition.

3. Add the vanilla and vinegar, then beat in the remaining sugar for 1 minute. You should still be able to feel grains of sugar in the mixture. Gently fold the cornflour through the meringue. Use a spatula to form the meringue into a circular shape on the prepared tray and bake for 55 minutes. Turn the oven off and leave the pavlova in there until cooled.

4. Dress with fresh whipped cream and your fruit of choice.

QUICK BANOFFEE PIES

MAKES 12

Caramel, banana and cream all come together
to create a delicious dessert that you will be
craving for days after eating.

INGREDIENTS

12 individual frozen shortcrust (pie) tart shells

2 × quantities Five-minute microwave Caramel Sauce (see page 230)

300 ml (10½ fl oz) thickened (whipping) cream, whipped

2 perfectly ripe bananas

1 Cadbury Flake chocolate bar, crumbled (if you can't find a Flake,
use 30 g (1 oz) milk chocolate shavings)

LET'S PUT IT ALL TOGETHER

1. Preheat the oven to 180°C (350°F). Bake the frozen tart shells
   for 10 minutes. Remove from the oven and allow to cool.
2. Spoon in the caramel sauce, then top with the whipped cream,
   a slice of banana and a sprinkle of crumbled chocolate. Repeat
   for all 12 tart shells.
3. You can prepare the tart shells and caramel filling ahead of time,
   then simply add the cream, banana and chocolate when you are
   ready to serve.

TIP Best eaten on the day of making.

HOMEMADE CHOCOLATE PUDDING

SERVES 4

This homemade version of a favourite snack food contains less sugar and no nasties. Serve with fresh berries or bananas for an easy and fun dessert.

INGREDIENTS
3 tablespoons cornflour (cornstarch)
2 tablespoons unsweetened cocoa powder
3 tablespoons sugar
600 ml (21 fl oz) milk

LET'S PUT IT ALL TOGETHER

1. Put all of the dry ingredients into a saucepan, add a little milk to start with and mix to a smooth paste.
2. Add the remaining milk, heat over low heat and stir constantly until thickened (about 5–10 minutes).
3. Turn off the heat, give a final stir, pour the chocolate mixture into moulds and allow to cool on the work surface before covering with plastic wrap and storing in the fridge.

CHERRY CHEESECAKE BALLS

This is a sneaky little dessert that's easy to make for when family or friends come over. I warn you, if you make them and you have no-one to share them with you may find yourself eating them all, they are that good. You will need a food processor for this recipe.

INGREDIENTS

125 g (4½ oz) Nice biscuits (sweet coconut-flavoured biscuits)
3 Cadbury Cherry Ripe chocolate bars (if you can't find these, use your favourite soft-centred chocolate bar), about 150 g (5½ oz)
250 g (9 oz) cream cheese

LET'S PUT IT ALL TOGETHER

1. Put the biscuits into the bowl of a food processor fitted with the metal chopping blade and process until a smooth crumb forms. Pour onto a plate. Give the food processor a wipe out with a clean cloth.
2. Break up the chocolate bars and place in the bowl of the food processor fitted with the metal chopping blade. Process until broken into crumbs. Add the cream cheese and process further until well combined.

3. Roll a tablespoon-size amount of the chocolate and cheese mixture into a ball. Gently roll the ball over the biscuit crumbs and place on a tray. Repeat until all the mixture is used.
4. Put the tray with the balls on it into the freezer for 30 minutes or until firm.
5. Enjoy straight away, or store in an airtight container in the fridge.

MARSHMALLOW, CARAMEL AND PEANUT BUTTER ROCKY ROAD

MAKES ABOUT 32 SERVES

This one is too good to save until Christmas;
it is a yummy treat at any time of year, really easy
to make and even easier to eat. It combines soft,
chewy and crunchy textures.

INGREDIENTS

400 g (14 oz) milk chocolate, broken into pieces
½ cup (125 g/4 oz) crunchy peanut butter
100 g (3½ oz) pink and white mini marshmallows
100 g (3½ oz) jersey caramels, cut into small pieces (if you can't
    find these, use caramel fudge or caramel creams instead)
100 g (3½ oz) plain sweet biscuits, crumbled into large chunks

LET'S PUT IT ALL TOGETHER

1. Line a 20 × 30-cm (8 × 12-inch) baking tin with baking paper.
2. Put the chocolate into a microwave-safe bowl, set the microwave to medium and heat for 30 seconds, stir, then return to the microwave for another 30 seconds. Repeat this process until the chocolate is melted and smooth.
3. Add the peanut butter to the chocolate and stir through.
4. Scatter the marshmallows, caramel pieces and biscuit chunks over the base of the lined tin, ensuring you get a good mixture all over.

5. Pour the melted chocolate mixture over, making sure to spread it evenly.
6. Transfer to the fridge for approximately 1 hour or, until set.
7. Cut into bite-size pieces.

FANTASTIC FUDGE

MAKES APPROXIMATELY 32 SERVES

Fudge is fantastic! With minimal ingredients and effort you can make a treat that no-one ever says no to. This is a great gift, wrapped up, for Easter or Christmas or served as treats at a birthday party.

INGREDIENTS

400 g (14 oz) milk chocolate, broken into pieces

395 g (14 oz) tin condensed milk

1 cup of chopped jersey caramels, crumbled biscuits, glacé cherries, nuts, or popcorn, for example (optional)

LET'S PUT IT ALL TOGETHER

1. Put the chocolate and condensed milk into a large microwave-safe bowl. Microwave on medium for 1 minute, then stir. Repeat this process until everything is melted and smooth.
2. If you are adding any of the optional ingredients to the fudge, do so now and stir through.
3. Pour the fudge mixture into a lined 20-cm (8-inch) square baking tin, smooth it out, then transfer to the fridge for a minimum of 2 hours or until set.
4. Cut into bite-size pieces to serve. Best enjoyed at room temperature.

YOGHURT PEANUT BUTTER DIP WITH APPLES

SERVES 4

This is a lovely sweet dip that makes an ideal healthier dessert option or afternoon snack. It is fun to eat and crazy easy to make. Switch the apples for your family's favourite fruits.

INGREDIENTS

4 tablespoons smooth peanut butter
200 g (7 oz) Greek yoghurt
1 tablespoon honey
2 apples, cored and cut into wedges, for dipping

LET'S PUT IT ALL TOGETHER

1. Put the peanut butter into a microwave-safe bowl. Microwave on medium for 15 seconds. You only want to soften it slightly to make it easier to mix in.
2. Add the yoghurt and honey to the peanut butter and stir until well combined.
3. Serve with apple slices or other fruits suitable for dipping.

ONE-MINUTE CHOCOLATE MUG CAKE

SERVES 1

Using your microwave, you can have a cake in your hand in just 1 minute. It sounds too good to be true, but it isn't. This is a fluffy chocolate cake that you can add ice cream and strawberries to if you like: a little indulgence in a mug.

INGREDIENTS

¼ cup (35 g/1¼ oz) self-raising flour
1 tablespoon unsweetened cocoa powder
1 tablespoon sugar
1 tablespoon butter, softened
¼ cup (60 ml/2 fl oz) milk
chocolate chips, for decorating

LET'S PUT IT ALL TOGETHER

1. Combine all of the ingredients except the chocolate chips in a mug. Mix well with a fork.
2. Sprinkle the chocolate chips on top and microwave on high for 1 minute.
3. Eat straight from the mug.

TIP Best enjoyed straight after making.

CARAMEL CREAMED RICE

SERVES 4

My mum used to always make creamed rice when we were growing up. She would sprinkle cinnamon on top and that was always my favourite part. I have taken her recipe and given it a little twist. Using brown sugar gives the creamed rice a lovely caramel flavour. Serve with fresh berries and whipped cream for extra indulgence or eat as is. You can reduce the sugar content to suit your taste.

INGREDIENTS

½ cup (110 g/3¾ oz) medium-grain rice
4 cups (1 litre/35 fl oz) milk (you can use low-fat milk)
⅓ cup (60 g/2¼ oz) brown sugar
1 teaspoon natural vanilla essence

LET'S PUT IT ALL TOGETHER

1. Wash the rice under running water and then drain.
2. Put the remaining ingredients in a heavy-based saucepan and bring to the boil.
3. Add the rice and reduce to a low simmer. Stir the rice through and then cover with a lid. Leave to cook for 45–50 minutes. You want almost all the milk to be absorbed. Stir occasionally while it cooks.
4. Enjoy warm or cold.

CHOCOLATE AND BERRY BREAD AND BUTTER PUDDING

SERVES 6–8

Bread and butter pudding doesn't have to be a plain dessert. You can make it look spectacular by adding chocolate (everyone's favourite) and mixed berries. This is a great winter dessert to make when you have a crowd to feed.

INGREDIENTS

50 g (1¾ oz) butter, melted
8 slices day-old bread
6 eggs
300 ml (10½ fl oz) thickened (whipping) cream
¼ cup (55 g/2 oz) caster (superfine) sugar
1 teaspoon natural vanilla essence
1 cup (125 g/4½ oz) frozen mixed berries
½ cup (75 g/2¾ oz) chocolate melts

LET'S PUT IT ALL TOGETHER

1. Preheat the oven to 180°C (350°F). Use a pastry brush to brush the melted butter on each side of the bread slices and inside the ovenproof dish you will be baking the pudding in.
2. Cut the bread slices into triangle quarters. Lay alternating triangles into the dish.
3. In a large bowl, lightly whisk the eggs with the cream, sugar and vanilla.

4. Pour the egg mixture over the bread in the dish, making sure to cover the bread evenly.
5. Top with the mixed berries and chocolate melts.
6. Allow to stand for 1 hour so that the bread can soak up the egg mixture.
7. Bake for 45–60 minutes until golden and the custard is just set.
8. Enjoy warm as is, or add extra berries, a drizzle of chocolate sauce and a scoop of ice cream.

UPSIDE-DOWN APPLE AND CINNAMON CAKE

SERVES 8–12

I love that an upside-down cake is already dressed
and requires no extra icing: it's good to go straight
from the oven. This upside-down apple cake is
best enjoyed warm with whipped cream,
making it a delicious dessert cake.

INGREDIENTS

125 g (4½ oz) butter, softened
½ cup (110 g/3¾ oz) caster (superfine) sugar
3 eggs
1 teaspoon natural vanilla essence
1 teaspoon ground cinnamon
1½ cups (225 g/8 oz) self-raising flour
¾ cup (150 g/5½ oz) brown sugar
400 g (14 oz) tin apple slices, drained
whipped cream, to serve

LET'S PUT IT ALL TOGETHER

1. Preheat the oven to 160°C (315°F). Line the base of a 20-cm
   (8-inch) round springform cake tin with baking paper.
2. Using a standing electric mixer fitted with the beater attachment
   or a handheld beater, beat the butter and caster sugar until light
   and creamy.

3. Add the eggs, one at a time, beating well after each addition. Add the vanilla, cinnamon and flour. Beat for a further minute until well combined. Spread the brown sugar over the bottom of the prepared tin, then lay the apple slices over the brown sugar.

4. Pour the cake batter over the apple and bake for 45–60 minutes. The cake is cooked when it bounces back when touched. Turn off the heat and allow the cake to cool in the oven for 5 minutes.

5. Remove from the oven and, placing a plate over the top of the tin, flip it over so the cake is now on the plate. Gently remove the tin from the cake and discard the baking paper.

6. Enjoy with whipped cream.

APPLE AND PEAR CRUMBLE

SERVES 8

You can't go wrong with a crumble—a delicious sweet base topped with a crunchy topping—it is a foolproof dish. I love to make crumble when I have a glut of apples and pears in my fruit bowl that need to be eaten.

INGREDIENTS

Topping

2 cups (200 g/7 oz) rolled (porridge) oats
¾ cup (65 g/2½ oz) desiccated (dried shredded) coconut
⅔ cup (100 g/3½ oz) plain (all-purpose) flour
1 teaspoon mixed (pumpkin pie) spice
½ cup (100 g/3½ oz) brown sugar
⅔ cup (170 ml/5½ fl oz) melted butter, margarine or olive oil spread

Filling

4 apples, peeled, cored and chopped
2 pears, peeled, cored and chopped
⅓ cup (100 g/3½ oz) brown sugar

LET'S PUT IT ALL TOGETHER

1. Preheat the oven to 160°C (315°F).
2. Put the ingredients for the filling in a saucepan over low heat and cook with the lid on until the apple and pear softens. Spoon into an ovenproof dish.

3. Combine all of the dry ingredients for the topping and then add the melted butter and mix well. Spread the crumble mixture over the cooked apple and pear mixture.
4. Bake for 15 minutes until the crumble is lightly golden.
5. Enjoy on its own or with ice cream or custard.

PEACH AND RASPBERRY COBBLER

SERVES 8+

What I love most about winter desserts is that you can pop them in the oven just as dinner is almost cooked and they will be ready after the tribe have eaten their dinner. This recipe for peach and raspberry cobbler is no exception, made in three easy steps. You'll be wanting to experiment with all types of fruit combinations. Try blueberries, apples, pears, apricots or mixed berries. When baked it gets a lovely rise with a crispy edge, a warm soft centre and the fruit waiting patiently on the bottom.

INGREDIENTS

125 g (4½ oz) butter, melted
200 g (7 oz) tinned peach slices, drained
1 cup (125 g/4½ oz) frozen raspberries
2 cups (300 g/10½ oz) self-raising flour
2 cups (500 ml/17 fl oz) milk (you can use low-fat milk if you prefer)
1½ cups (330 g/11¾ oz) sugar (if serving with ice cream or custard, you could use 1 cup (220 g/7¾ oz) sugar)

LET'S PUT IT ALL TOGETHER

1. Preheat the oven to 180°C (350°F).
2. Lay the peach slices and raspberries in the bottom of a 24-cm (9½-inch) pie dish and then pour the melted butter over.

3. In a bowl, mix together the flour, milk and sugar to form a smooth batter. Pour the batter over the fruit in the dish. Bake for 45–55 minutes until the batter rises and turns a lovely golden colour.
4. Serve with custard, ice cream or cream. Store any leftovers, covered, in the fridge and reheat prior to eating.

CHOCOLATE SELF-SAUCING PUDDING

SERVES APPROXIMATELY 6

A deliciously easy winter dessert, this dense chocolate pudding makes its own sauce as it cooks. Perfect to enjoy with ice cream or cream.

INGREDIENTS

1 cup (150 g/5½ oz) self-raising flour
½ teaspoon salt
2 tablespoons unsweetened cocoa powder
½ cup (110 g/3¾ oz) sugar
½ cup (125 ml/4 fl oz) milk
1 teaspoon natural vanilla essence
1 tablespoon butter, melted

Sauce

½ cup (100 g/3½ oz) brown sugar
¼ cup (30 g/1 oz) unsweetened cocoa powder
1¾ cups (435 ml/15¼ fl oz) hot water

LET'S PUT IT ALL TOGETHER

1. Preheat the oven to 180°C (350°F). Grease and line a 20-cm (8-inch) round cake tin or baking dish.
2. Put the flour, salt, cocoa and sugar into a bowl. Mix to combine. Add the milk, vanilla and melted butter and stir until smooth. Spread evenly into the prepared tin.
3. Sprinkle the brown sugar and cocoa for the sauce over the pudding. Gently pour the hot water over the top.
4. Bake for 45 minutes until you have a cake like centre and chocolate sauce around it.
5. Serve with cream or ice cream.

CHOCOLATE AND RASPBERRY BROWNIES

MAKES 12

These brownies are so quick and easy to make, they will become a family favourite in no time. They have a lovely dense chocolate centre with bursts of tangy raspberries.

INGREDIENTS

125 g (4½ oz) butter, chopped
2 cups (300 g/10½ oz) chopped milk or dark chocolate
½ cup (100 g/3½ oz) brown sugar
2 teaspoons natural vanilla essence
2 eggs
1 cup (150 g/5½ oz) plain (all-purpose) flour
1 cup (125 g/4½ oz) frozen raspberries
icing (confectioners') sugar, to serve
fresh raspberries, to serve

LET'S PUT IT ALL TOGETHER

1. Preheat the oven to 180°C (350°F). Grease and line a 12-hole standard muffin tin or 18 cm × 32-cm (7 × 12½-inch) baking tin.
2. In a small saucepan, melt the butter and chocolate over low heat, stirring occasionally until smooth. Remove the saucepan from the heat and allow to cool slightly.
3. Add the brown sugar and vanilla to the chocolate mixture, followed by the eggs, and stir until combined.
4. Stir the flour through, then fold through the raspberries until just combined.

5. Pour the chocolate mixture into the prepared tin and bake for 30 minutes or until set. Allow to cool slightly in the tin and then remove (cut into 12 pieces if you have not used a muffin tin) and serve with a generous dusting of icing sugar and some fresh raspberries.

BLUEBERRY AND WHITE CHOCOLATE BLONDIES

MAKES 16

A blondie is a brownie's fairer sister and is perfect for white-chocolate lovers: the addition of blueberries adds a lovely fresh burst of colour and flavour.

INGREDIENTS

½ cup (110 g/3¾ oz) sugar

3 eggs

1 teaspoon natural vanilla essence

1½ cups (225 g/8 oz) plain (all-purpose) flour

1 teaspoon baking powder

125 g (4½ oz) butter, melted

1 cup (150 g/5½ oz) white chocolate buttons

½ cup (80 g/2¾ oz) (fresh or frozen) blueberries

LET'S PUT IT ALL TOGETHER

1. Preheat the oven to 180°C (350°F). Line a 24-cm (9½-inch) loaf tin with baking paper.
2. Put the sugar, eggs and vanilla into a large mixing bowl and whisk well to combine. Add the flour and baking powder and mix well.
3. Pour the melted butter into the egg mixture and add the white chocolate buttons. Mix well.
4. Spread the batter into the prepared tin and then scatter the blueberries on top. Bake for 30 minutes or until the blondie is lightly golden and bounces back when touched.

5. Allow to cool in the tin for 5 minutes and then turn out onto a wire rack. Slice into 16 pieces.
6. Best enjoyed at room temperature.

HOMEMADE MARSHMALLOWS WITH HONEY

MAKES 50+

What kid doesn't love marshmallows? Actually, what adult doesn't love marshmallows? They are squishy sweet goodness and you can never possibly stop at one. These marshmallows are made with honey, which has a lower glycaemic index than sugar.

INGREDIENTS

1 cup (250 ml/8 fl oz) water
1 cup (350 g/12 oz) honey
1 teaspoon natural vanilla essence
¼ teaspoon salt
3 tablespoons powdered gelatine
2 cups (180 g/6¼ oz) desiccated (dried shredded) coconut and
    2 drops of red food colouring (optional)

LET'S PUT IT ALL TOGETHER

1. In a small saucepan over medium heat, combine ½ cup (125 ml/4 fl oz) of the water with the honey, vanilla and salt. Heat for about 10 minutes until the mixture reaches a soft-ball consistency. This is when it easily coats the back of the spoon and if you were to drop a small amount into a glass of cold water it would stay together in a semiformed mass. You don't want it to form a hard mass: this means it has cooked too long. Another indication it's ready is that when you're stirring the mix in the saucepan it will start to slightly come away from the sides.

2. In the bowl of a standing electric mixer fitted with the whisk attachment, combine the remaining ½ cup (125 ml/4 fl oz) of water with the gelatine. Do this step just before you are ready to add the hot mixture. Turn the mixer on low speed and slowly pour the hot ingredients into the bowl.

3. When all of the mixture has been added, increase the speed to high and whisk for 10 minutes until you have a large white mass that resembles marshmallow.

4. If you want to coat the marshmallows in coconut, put the coconut in a resealable plastic bag and add the food colouring. Mix through by rolling the sides of the bag between your hands to get an even coverage.

5. Line a baking tray with baking paper and spread half of the coconut (if using) evenly over the tray.

6. When removing the marshmallow mixture from the bowl, spoon out as much as you can onto the tray. Then wet your hands with a little water and push the mix into shape. Spread the remaining coconut on top and leave to set on the workbench for 30 minutes.

7. Remove the marshmallow from the tray by lifting the baking paper. Transfer to a cutting board and cut into the size you like. When cutting, roll the uncoated edges in the coconut that remains.

8. Store in an airtight container for up to 2 weeks.

 TIP Why not try adding peppermint essence or rosewater to the marshmallow? Add a few drops of food colouring to the mix for coloured marshmallow.

RASPBERRY BUBBLE JELLY

MAKES 10 SMALL CUPS

Real raspberries and sparkling raspberry soft drink (carbonated drink) go into this jelly to give it a noticeable bubbly texture on the tongue when eaten.

INGREDIENTS

250 g (9 oz) frozen raspberries, plus extra for decoration
1 heaped tablespoon powdered gelatine
1½ cups (375 ml/13 fl oz) raspberry-flavoured soft drink
(carbonated drink)

LET'S PUT IT ALL TOGETHER

1. Put the frozen raspberries and 215 ml (7½ fl oz) of water in a small saucepan over medium heat and stir for about 1 minute until the raspberries soften. Remove from the heat and transfer to a food processor. Process for 30 seconds or to a smooth consistency.
2. Press the raspberry purée through a sieve to remove the seeds.
3. Take ½ cup (125 ml/4 fl oz) of the warm raspberry purée and stir in the powdered gelatine. Return this to the remaining raspberry purée in the food processor and process for 10 seconds. Add the raspberry soft drink and mix through.
4. Pour into small moulds (I use disposable shot cups) and refrigerate for 2 hours. Top with extra frozen raspberries.

NOTE If you choose to pour the jelly into one large mould you will need to refrigerate it for a minimum of 4 hours.

STRAWBERRY AND YOGHURT ICE CREAMS

MAKES 6

One thing I love doing during the warmer months
is making my own ice creams for the kids. I enjoy
experimenting with different fruits, yoghurt, creams and
so on. This is the latest creation I have made: they are
fantastic for cooling down and you know exactly
what the kids are eating.

INGREDIENTS

250 g (9 oz) strawberries, hulled
½ cup (130 g/4½ oz) plain yoghurt
¼ cup (60 ml/2 fl oz) thickened (whipping) cream
3 tablespoons sweetened condensed milk

LET'S PUT IT ALL TOGETHER

1. Using a blender, food processor or personal blender, process all of the ingredients (reserving two strawberries, sliced, for decoration) until smooth.
2. Pour the mixture into ice-cream moulds. Before putting the top on, slide in a slice of strawberry on the side of each mould. Put the lid on and freeze for a minimum of 4 hours.

REAL FRUIT ICE BLOCKS

MAKES 6+

Real fruit ice blocks (popsicles/ice lollies) are so easy to
make and are perfect for using up fruit that still tastes
good, although it may have lost its visual appeal.
Grab that fruit and a blender and make some yummy
fruity ice creations.

INGREDIENTS

fresh fruit, peeled, deseeded and chopped: I use watermelon and
blueberries

LET'S PUT IT ALL TOGETHER

1. Simply put the fruit in a blender and process until smooth.
   Some fruit may require a little added water to get to a pouring
   consistency.
2. Pour into ice-cream moulds. You can do layers, as I have, if you
   have a little more time.
3. Put the moulds in the freezer for a minimum of 4 hours.

 TIP Other fruits that work well are stone fruits,
mangoes, pineapple, kiwifruit, strawberries and
raspberries.

MANGO, COCONUT AND MACADAMIA NUT ICE CREAMS

MAKES 6

If you love the tropical combo of mango and coconut, then you will absolutely love these ice creams. They are filled with no nasties and are perfect for all the family.

INGREDIENTS

½ cup (75 g/2¾ oz) macadamia nuts
2 over-ripe mangoes, peeled and seed removed
⅓ cup (90 g/3¼ oz) coconut cream

LET'S PUT IT ALL TOGETHER

1. Put the macadamia nuts into the bowl of a food processor fitted with the metal chopping blade and process the nuts into small pieces.
2. Add the mango flesh and coconut cream to the food processor and process until combined.
3. Pour into ice-cream moulds and freeze for a minimum of 4 hours.

snack Attack

You'll have morning tea, afternoon tea and school-lunchbox fillers sorted with these delicious and easy slices, muffins, biscuits (cookies), breads and more.

ORANGE, CHOC-CHIP AND BLACK CHIA SEED BISCUITS

MAKES 20

With a lovely chocolate–orange flavour and the added
bonus of the vitamins and minerals from the black chia
seeds, these cookies will be devoured in no time,
trust me: I have to hide them when I make them
or they are all gone in one afternoon!

INGREDIENTS

125 g (4½ oz) butter, cubed and softened
¾ cup (165 g/5¾ oz) caster (superfine) sugar
1 egg
finely grated zest of 1 orange
1½ cups (225 g/8 oz) plain (all-purpose) flour
1 teaspoon baking powder
½ cup (85 g/3 oz) chocolate chips
3 tablespoons black chia seeds (white are fine, but you won't
   see them)

LET'S PUT IT ALL TOGETHER

1. Preheat the oven to 180°C (350°F). Line a baking tray with
   baking paper and set aside.
2. Using a standing electric mixer fitted with the beater attachment,
   or a handheld beater, cream together the butter and sugar. Add
   the egg and orange zest and beat until combined.
3. Add the flour, baking powder, chocolate chips and chia seeds and
   mix until it comes together into a firm biscuit (cookie) dough.

4. Roll tablespoon-size amounts and flatten them on the prepared tray, leaving about 2 cm (¾ inch) space between each biscuit to allow for spreading when baking.
5. Bake for 10–15 minutes, until lightly golden around the edges. Cool on a wire rack.

WHITE CHOCOLATE BISCUITS

MAKES 12

White chocolate is sometimes overlooked for its darker competition, milk chocolate; however, in these cookies white chocolate is the star. Add some macadamia nuts and you have a decadent treat.

INGREDIENTS

125 g (4½ oz) butter, softened
½ cup (110 g/3¾ oz) caster (superfine) sugar
1 teaspoon natural vanilla essence
1 egg, lightly beaten
1½ cups (225 g/8 oz) self-raising flour
125 g (4½ oz) white chocolate chips
½ cup (60 g/2¼ oz) roughly chopped macadamia nuts (optional)

LET'S PUT IT ALL TOGETHER

1. Preheat the oven to 180°C (350°F). Line a baking tray with baking paper and set aside.

2. Using a standing electric mixer fitted with the beater attachment, or a handheld beater, beat together the butter, sugar and vanilla until light and creamy. Gradually add the egg and beat well to combine. Fold in the self-raising flour and white chocolate chips and macadamias (if using).

3. Place tablespoon-size amounts of the dough on the prepared tray, leaving about 2 cm (¾ inch) between each biscuit to allow for spreading when baking. Bake for 15 minutes or until lightly golden.

4. Allow to cool on the tray before transferring to a wire rack.

OAT AND SULTANA BISCUITS

MAKES 12

These biscuits (cookies) could almost pass as breakfast.
Filled with oats and sultanas (golden raisins) and
sweetened with honey, they are great with a glass of
cold milk or a cup of tea.

INGREDIENTS

125 g (4½ oz) butter
½ cup (175 g/6 oz) honey
1 cup (95 g/3¼ oz) rolled (porridge) oats
1 cup (150 g/5½ oz) self-raising flour
½ cup (85 g/3 oz) sultanas (golden raisins)

LET'S PUT IT ALL TOGETHER

1. Preheat the oven to 180°C (350°F). Line a baking tray with baking paper and set aside.
2. Put the butter and honey in a microwave-safe bowl. Microwave on high for 45 seconds or until the butter is melted.
3. Add the rolled oats, flour and sultanas to the melted butter mixture and stir well to combine.
4. Place tablespoon-size amounts of dough on the prepared tray, leaving about 2 cm (¾ inch) space between each biscuit to allow for spreading when baking.
5. Bake for 15 minutes or until lightly golden.
6. Allow to cool on the tray before transferring to a wire rack.

FUDGY CHOCOLATE COOKIES

MAKES 24

As the name suggests, these cookies (biscuits) have a fudgy centre and crisp edge. They are a complete indulgence: store them on a high shelf in the pantry, or there will be none left when you want one.

INGREDIENTS

125 g (4½ oz) butter, softened
½ cup (110 g/3¾ oz) sugar
½ cup (100 g/3½ oz) brown sugar
1 egg
1 teaspoon natural vanilla essence
1 cup (150 g/5½ oz) plain (all-purpose) flour
½ cup (55 g/2 oz) unsweetened cocoa powder
1 teaspoon baking powder
2 tablespoons milk
1 cup (170 g/6 oz) chocolate chips

LET'S PUT IT ALL TOGETHER

1. Using a standing electric mixer fitted with the beater attachment, or a handheld beater, beat the butter in a bowl for 20 seconds. Add both the sugar and brown sugar and continue beating on medium speed until light and creamy.
2. Add the egg and vanilla to the butter mixture and continue beating, scraping down the side of the bowl as you go.
3. Turn the beater off and add the flour, cocoa and baking powder. Mix slowly to combine well.

4. Add the milk and chocolate chips to the mixture and fold through gently. The dough will be really sticky and needs to be refrigerated for a minimum of 2 hours before rolling into balls. (The dough can be refrigerated for up to 36 hours until you are ready to use it.)
5. Preheat the oven to 180°C (350°F). Line a baking tray with baking paper.
6. Roll tablespoon-size amounts of dough into balls and place them on the prepared tray, leaving 2 cm between each ball, repeating until all of the dough is used.
7. Bake for 15 minutes. After about 10 minutes, take the tray out of the oven and gently flatten the biscuits (be careful, as they are hot), then return them to the oven for the remaining cooking time. Allow to cool on the tray before transferring to a wire rack.

JAM DROPS

MAKES 20–24

For decades, these simple biscuits (cookies) have been a favourite in many families. They show up regularly at school fêtes, fundraisers and on your grandma's kitchen table.

INGREDIENTS

125 g (4½ oz) butter, softened
¾ cup (150 g/5½ oz) brown sugar
1 teaspoon natural vanilla essence
1 egg
1 cup (150 g/5½ oz) plain (all-purpose) flour
½ cup (75 g/2¾ oz) self-raising flour
strawberry jam, or your favourite flavour

LET'S PUT IT ALL TOGETHER

1. Preheat the oven to 180°C (350°F). Line a baking tray with baking paper and set aside.
2. Using a standing electric mixer fitted with the beater attachment, or a handheld beater, beat the butter, brown sugar and vanilla. Add the egg and continue to beat until well combined. Add the plain and self-raising flours and mix until a dough forms.
3. Take tablespoon-size amounts, roll into a ball, and place on the prepared tray. Repeat until all of the dough is used.
4. Using your thumb, push down on the balls to make an indent in the middle. Fill the indent with a drop of the strawberry jam (or your favourite jam).
5. Bake for 10 minutes or until lightly golden. Transfer to a wire rack to cool.

CHEWY CHOC-CHIP BISCUITS

MAKES 30

....

Get back to basics and make some easy and tasty treats
to fill the lunchbox, have on hand or stock up the freezer.
Choc-chip biscuits are an all-time favourite in many
households: the kids love the chocolate chips and I love
the fact that I have made them, knowing each and every
ingredient I have added.

....

INGREDIENTS

125 g (4½ oz) butter, cubed
¾ cup (150 g/5½ oz) brown sugar
¼ cup (55 g/2 oz) caster (superfine) sugar
1 egg
1 teaspoon natural vanilla essence
1 cup (150 g/5½ oz) plain (all-purpose) flour
1 cup (150 g/5½ oz) self-raising flour
1 teaspoon baking powder
1 cup (170 g/6 oz) chocolate chips

LET'S PUT IT ALL TOGETHER

1. Preheat the oven to 180°C (350°F). Line a baking tray with
   baking paper and set aside.
2. In a medium microwave-safe bowl, melt the butter in the
   microwave on medium–high for 45 seconds (every microwave
   is different, so check at 20-second intervals).
3. Add the brown sugar and caster sugar to the melted butter and
   mix well.

4. In a separate bowl, lightly whisk the egg and then whisk it into the butter and sugar mixture. Add the vanilla and mix well. The mixture will look like caramel. Add the plain and self-raising flours and baking powder and stir to combine. Fold through the chocolate chips.
5. Roll the dough into balls and place on the prepared tray. Repeat until all the dough is used. Bake for 12–15 minutes or until lightly golden. Cool on a wire rack.

CHEESE BISCUIT BITES

MAKES 100+

These are a great alternative to store-bought biscuit (cracker) snacks. For lunchboxes or days out, a serving of about 10 of these mini bites in a resealable plastic bag or small airtight container makes an easy homemade snack. The recipe is so easy with only five ingredients: a batch makes about a hundred bite-size biscuits, so you will have a week's worth done in no time.

INGREDIENTS

1 cup plain (all-purpose) flour
1 teaspoon salt
50 g (1¾ oz) butter, chilled and cubed
2 cups (200 g/7 oz) grated cheddar cheese
3–4 tablespoons iced water

LET'S PUT IT ALL TOGETHER

1. Preheat the oven to 180°C (350°F). Line a baking tray with baking paper and set aside.
2. Use a food processor or in a bowl, process or rub together the flour, salt and butter until the mixture resembles breadcrumbs.
3. Add the cheese and the water, a tablespoon at a time, with the food processor on or kneading by hand to form a nice dough ball. It shouldn't be sticky. If it's sticky, add a little more flour.

4. Transfer the dough to a floured surface and roll it out with a rolling pin until about 2–3 mm (⅛ inch) thick. Cut out shapes with mini cookie cutters or cut into small squares.
5. Place the shapes on the prepared tray and bake for 10–12 minutes until lightly golden. Transfer to a wire rack and allow to completely cool before storing.

LATTE BISCUITS

MAKES 20

If coffee is your thing, then these biscuits (cookies) are for you. Enjoy your morning cuppa with a coffee-flavoured biscuit and have a double hit.

INGREDIENTS

½ cup (110 g/3¾ oz) sugar
½ cup (100 g/3½ oz) brown sugar
⅓ cup (90 g/3¼ oz) softened butter
1 teaspoon natural vanilla essence
1 egg
2 tablespoons instant coffee powder
1 tablespoon boiling water
1½ cups (225 g/8 oz) plain (all-purpose) flour
½ teaspoon baking powder
½ teaspoon bicarbonate of soda (baking soda)

LET'S PUT IT ALL TOGETHER

1. Preheat the oven to 180°C (350°F). Line a baking tray with baking paper and set aside.
2. Using a standing electric mixer fitted with the beater attachment or a handheld electric beater, combine the sugar and brown sugar, butter and vanilla until light and creamy. Add the egg and continue to beat until well combined.
3. In a cup, dissolve the coffee in the boiling water. Alternatively, if you have an espresso machine you can make a shot of espresso.

4. Add the coffee to the mixture in the bowl and stir until combined. Add the flour, baking powder and bicarbonate soda and mix to combine and form a dough.
5. Place teaspoon-size amounts of the dough on the prepared tray, leaving enough room between each one for them to expand as they bake.
6. Bake for 12–15 minutes until the biscuits are lightly golden. Allow to cool on the tray before transferring to a wire rack.

BANANA AND CHOC-CHIP MUFFINS

MAKES 12

I love one-bowl recipes as they are simple to make and require less washing up. These muffins will be in the oven in no time. A classic banana flavour with bursts of chocolate chips.

INGREDIENTS

2 over-ripe bananas, mashed
2 eggs
½ cup (125 ml/4 fl oz) sunflower oil
½ cup (110 g/3¾ oz) sugar
1½ cups (225 g/8 oz) self-raising flour
1 teaspoon bicarbonate of soda (baking soda)
¼ cup (60 ml/2 fl oz) milk
½ cup (85 g/3 oz) chocolate chips

LET'S PUT IT ALL TOGETHER

1. Preheat the oven to 180°C (350°F). Place paper muffin cases in a 12-hole standard muffin tin and set aside.
2. Put the bananas, eggs, oil and sugar into a large bowl and mix together. Add the remaining ingredients and mix until combined.
3. Divide the mixture evenly between the paper cases in the tin. Bake for 15 minutes or until the muffins bounce back when touched. Allow to cool in the tin for 5 minutes, then transfer to a wire rack to cool completely before storing.

BANANA, BLUEBERRY AND OAT MUFFINS

MAKES 12

With its delicious banana flavour, a burst of blueberries plus wholesome oats, this muffin is perfect for breakfast and the school lunchbox.

INGREDIENTS

1⅔ cups (250 g/9 oz) plain (all-purpose) flour
1 cup (105 g/3½ oz) instant oats
½ cup (100 g/3½ oz) brown sugar
3 teaspoons baking powder
1 teaspoon ground cinnamon
1 teaspoon salt
2 eggs, separated
1 cup (155 g/5½ oz) blueberries, fresh or frozen
2 ripe bananas, mashed
3 tablespoons vegetable oil
1 cup (250 ml/9 fl oz) milk

LET'S PUT IT ALL TOGETHER

1. Preheat the oven to 180°C (350°F). Place paper muffin cases in a 12-hole standard muffin tin and set aside.
2. Put the dry ingredients (flour, oats, sugar, baking powder, cinnamon and salt) into a large mixing bowl. Add the egg yolks to the dry mix and, in a separate bowl, whisk the egg whites until frothy and set aside.

3. Add all the remaining wet ingredients to the egg yolk mixture and mix to combine.
4. Fold in the egg whites.
5. Spoon into the paper cases in the prepared tin. Bake for 15 minutes or until the muffins bounce back when touched. Allow to cool in the tin for 5 minutes, then transfer to a wire rack to cool completely before storing.

CHOCOLATE AND ZUCCHINI MUFFINS

MAKES 12

These chocolate and zucchini muffins are a marvellous vegie smuggler. Green vegetables are currently a no-go in our house, noses turned up and all. So instead of battling over something that they will eventually grow out of, I'm sneaking them into all sorts of meals.

INGREDIENTS

1 zucchini (courgette), grated
1¾ cups (260 g/9¼ oz) self-raising flour
200 ml (7 fl oz) milk
2 eggs
80 g (2¾ oz) butter, melted
1 teaspoon natural vanilla essence
80 g (2¾ oz) raw (unrefined) sugar
35 g (1¼ oz) unsweetened cocoa powder

LET'S PUT IT ALL TOGETHER

1. Preheat the oven to 180°C (350°F). Place paper muffin cases in a 12-hole standard muffin tin and set aside.
2. Simply combine all the ingredients in a large bowl and stir gently. You don't want to overwork the batter.

3. Spoon the batter into the prepared tin. Bake for 15 minutes or until the muffins bounce back when touched. Allow to cool in the tin for 5 minutes, then transfer to a wire rack to cool completely before storing.

CHOC-CHIP MUFFINS

MAKES 12

Another back-to-basics classic: you could swap the chocolate chips for other favourites such as frozen berries, white chocolate, sultanas (golden raisins) and so on. They are freezer-friendly and absolutely delicious (you will have to cover them up while they cool, or little hands may grab one).

INGREDIENTS

2½ cups (225 g/8 oz) self-raising flour
½ cup (110 g/3¾ oz) caster (superfine) sugar
1 cup (170 g/6 oz) chocolate chips
1¼ cups (310 ml/10¾ fl oz) milk
1 teaspoon natural vanilla essence
1 egg
2 tablespoons melted butter (or you can use coconut oil)

LET'S PUT IT ALL TOGETHER

1. Preheat the oven to 180°C (350°F). Place paper muffin cases in a 12-hole standard muffin tin and set aside.
2. Put the flour, sugar and chocolate chips in a large bowl and mix to combine.
3. In a jug, measure the milk, then add the vanilla, egg and melted butter (or coconut oil). Whisk to combine.

4. Pour the milk mixture into the dry ingredients and stir with a spoon until just combined.

5. Spoon the batter into the prepared muffin tin. Bake for 20 minutes or until the muffins bounce back when touched. Allow to cool in the tin for 5 minutes, then transfer to a wire rack to cool completely before storing.

STRAWBERRY-JAM CENTRED WHITE CHOC-CHIP MUFFINS

MAKES 12

When you bite into these muffins you are greeted by
a strawberry jam filling, and then the white-chocolate
flavour comes through the muffin, which makes them just
lovely. Try experimenting with different kinds of jam and
you will have many different muffins at your fingertips.
This recipe is an easy three-step process and littlies
can help, as it is all mixed by hand and there are
no hot ingredients to add.

INGREDIENTS

2 cups (300 g/10½ oz) self-raising flour
½ cup (110 g/3¾ oz) sugar
2 eggs
1 cup (250 ml/9 fl oz) milk
100 ml (3½ fl oz) olive oil
1 teaspoon natural vanilla essence
½ cup (85 g/3 oz) white chocolate chips
12 teaspoons strawberry jam or conserve

LET'S PUT IT ALL TOGETHER

1. Preheat the oven to 180°C (350°F). Place paper muffin cases in
   a 12-hole standard muffin tin and set aside.
2. Combine all of the ingredients except the white chocolate chips
   and strawberry jam in a large bowl and whisk together well.

3. Fold through the white chocolate chips. Spoon into the paper cases, only to just over halfway.

4. Spoon 1 teaspoon of strawberry jam on top of the mix for each muffin.

5. Bake for 20 minutes or until the muffins bounce back when touched. Allow to cool in the tin for 5 minutes, then transfer to a wire rack to cool completely before eating.

CARROT, APPLE AND BRAN MUFFINS

MAKES 12

Vegetables and fruit come together in this delicious muffin. Packed with fibre and goodness these are great for a quick breakfast or school lunchbox.

INGREDIENTS

2 cups (300 g/10½ oz) plain (all-purpose) flour
2 teaspoons baking powder
½ teaspoon bicarbonate of soda (baking soda)
½ cup (100 g/3½ oz) brown sugar
½ teaspoon ground cinnamon
½ cup (35 g/1¼ oz) unprocessed bran
1 carrot, grated
1 Granny Smith apple, grated
2 eggs
½ cup (125 ml/4 fl oz) sunflower oil
½ cup (125 ml/4 fl oz) milk

LET'S PUT IT ALL TOGETHER

1. Preheat the oven to 180°C (350°F). Place paper muffin cases in a 12-hole standard muffin tin and set aside.
2. Put the flour, baking powder, bicarbonate of soda, brown sugar, cinnamon and bran into a large bowl and mix to combine.
3. Add the grated carrot and apple to the dry mixture and toss through.

4. In a jug, whisk together the eggs, sunflower oil and milk and then add to the mixture in the bowl. Stir until just combined.
5. Spoon the batter into the prepared muffin tin. Bake for 15–20 minutes or until the muffins bounce back when touched. Allow to cool in the tin for 5 minutes, then transfer to a wire rack to cool completely before storing.

DOUBLE CHOCOLATE MUFFINS

MAKES 12

Chocolate, chocolate and more chocolate: that is the best way to describe these muffins. Each bite is bursting with chocolate chunks in a fluffy chocolate muffin.

INGREDIENTS

125 g (4½ oz) butter, softened
⅔ cup (150 g/5½ oz) caster (superfine) sugar
1 egg
2 cups (300 g/10½ oz) self-raising flour
½ cup (55 g/2 oz) unsweetened cocoa powder
1½ cups (375 ml/13 fl oz) milk
1 cup (170 g/6 oz) milk chocolate chips
½ cup (85 g/3 oz) dark chocolate chips

LET'S PUT IT ALL TOGETHER

1. Preheat the oven to 180°C (350°F). Place paper muffin cases in a 12-hole standard muffin tin and set aside.
2. Put the butter and sugar into the bowl of a standing electric mixer fitted with the beater attachment, or use a handheld beater, and beat until creamy. Add the egg and beat until well combined.
3. Add the flour, cocoa, milk and chocolate chips (reserve a few chocolate chips for decorating the top of the muffins) to the egg mixture and fold through until combined. Don't overmix.

4. Spoon the batter into the prepared muffin tin. Sprinkle the reserved chocolate chips on top. Bake for 15–20 minutes or until the muffins bounce back when touched. Allow to cool in the tin for 5 minutes, then transfer to a wire rack to cool completely before storing.

LEMON AND POPPY SEED MUFFINS

MAKES 12

This muffin recipe is dedicated to my mum, who is called Poppy. These muffins have a fresh lemon zing and are drizzled with a lemon icing (frosting).

INGREDIENTS

125 g (4½ oz) butter, softened
⅔ cup (150 g/5½ oz) caster (superfine) sugar
2 eggs
2½ cups (375 g/13 oz) self-raising flour
2 tablespoons poppy seeds
1½ cups (375 ml/13 fl oz) buttermilk*
finely grated zest of 1 lemon

Icing
1 cup (125 g/4½ oz) icing (confectioners') sugar
2 tablespoons lemon juice

LET'S PUT IT ALL TOGETHER

1. Preheat the oven to 180°C (350°F). Place paper muffin cases in a 12-hole standard muffin tin and set aside.
2. Put the butter and sugar into the bowl of a standing electric mixer fitted with the beater attachment, or use a handheld beater, and beat until creamy. Add the eggs, one at a time, beating well after each addition.
3. Add the flour, poppy seeds, buttermilk and lemon zest to the egg mixture and beat until combined.

4. Spoon the batter into the prepared muffin tin. Bake for 15–20 minutes or until the muffins bounce back when touched. Allow to cool in the tin for 5 minutes, then transfer to a wire rack to cool completely before icing.

5. To make the icing: mix together the icing sugar and lemon juice in a bowl.

6. When the muffins have cooled, drizzle the icing over the top.

*TIP Make your own buttermilk by combining 1½ cups (375 ml/13 fl oz) of milk with 1½ tablespoons of lemon juice or white vinegar. Stand for 5 minutes before using.

PIZZA MUFFINS

Here are all your favourite pizza flavours in a muffin.
These make a great lunch on-the-go as they are quick
and easy to eat. Have some ready in the freezer for
times when you need a quick bite. Leave the
ham out for a vegetarian option.

INGREDIENTS

2 cups (300 g/10½ oz) self-raising flour
1 tablespoon dried Italian herbs
1 cup (135 g/4¾ oz) peeled and grated zucchini (courgette)
1 cup (100 g/3½ oz) grated tasty cheddar cheese
1 cup (155 g/5½ oz) coarsely chopped ham
¼ cup (30 g/1 oz) thinly sliced black olives
¼ cup (40 g/1½ oz) coarsely chopped sundried tomatoes
2 eggs
1 cup (250 ml/9 fl oz) milk

LET'S PUT IT ALL TOGETHER

1. Preheat the oven to 180°C (350°F). Place paper muffin cases in a 12-hole standard muffin tin and set aside.
2. Put the flour, dried herbs, zucchini and cheese in a large bowl and stir well to coat the zucchini and cheese. Add the ham, olives and sundried tomatoes and mix to combine.

3. Add the eggs and milk to the flour mixture and stir until all the flour is mixed in. Don't overmix, or the muffins will be tough.

4. Spoon the batter into the prepared muffin tin. Bake for 15–20 minutes or until the muffins bounce back when touched. Allow to cool in the tin for 5 minutes, then transfer to a wire rack to cool completely before storing.

THE BEST BANANA CHOC-CHIP BREAD

MAKES 1 LOAF (ABOUT 10 SLICES)

Yes, this is the best banana choc-chip bread you will ever make, full of banana and bursting with chocolate chips. Bake it in a narrow loaf tin for best results.

INGREDIENTS

100 g (3½ oz) light olive oil spread, at room temperature

3 over-ripe bananas

2 eggs

½ cup (110 g/3¾ oz) raw (unrefined) sugar

1 teaspoon natural vanilla essence

1 cup (150 g/5½ oz) large chocolate melts (I use the larger Nestlé melts)

2½ cups (375 g/13 oz) plain (all-purpose) flour

2 teaspoons baking powder

LET'S PUT IT ALL TOGETHER

1. Preheat the oven to 180°C (350°F). Line a 20 × 10-cm (8 × 4-inch) loaf tin with baking paper and set aside.
2. In a large bowl, put the olive oil spread and bananas and mash with a fork. Add the eggs, raw sugar and vanilla. Whisk to combine the ingredients really well.
3. Add the chocolate melts, reserving 5 for decoration, followed by the plain flour and baking powder to the egg mixture. Continue to whisk until the flour is just combined.

4. Spoon the bread batter into the prepared loaf tin. Place the reserved chocolate melts in a line down the centre and bake for 30–40 minutes until the bread is lightly golden and it bounces back when touched.

5. Allow to cool in the tin for 5 minutes before turning out onto a wire rack to cool completely.

TIP Best consumed within 3 days of baking or slice and freeze individual portions for school lunchboxes.

STRAWBERRY BREAD

MAKES I LOAF (ABOUT 10 SLICES)

Make the most of strawberry season with this bread.
The flavour and aroma of cinnamon complements the
strawberries in each slice. Enjoy as is, or toast and smear
with a little butter for a quick breakfast option.

INGREDIENTS

125 g (4½ oz) butter, softened
¾ cup (150 g/5½ oz) brown sugar
I teaspoon natural vanilla essence
3 eggs
2 cups (300 g/10½ oz) self-raising flour
½ teaspoon bicarbonate of soda (baking soda)
I teaspoon ground cinnamon
½ cup (125 g/4½ oz) sour cream
1½ cups (225 g/8 oz) sliced strawberries

LET'S PUT IT ALL TOGETHER

1. Preheat the oven to 180°C (350°F). Line a 24 × 14-cm
   (9½ × 5½-inch) loaf tin with baking paper and set aside.
2. In the bowl of a standing electric mixer fitted with the beater
   attachment, or using a handheld electric beater, beat together
   the butter, sugar and vanilla until creamy. Add the eggs, one at a
   time, beating well after each addition.
3. Add the flour, bicarbonate of soda, cinnamon and sour cream to
   the egg mixture and beat until combined.
4. Fold the strawberries through the batter.

5. Spoon the batter into the prepared tin and bake for about 50 minutes until the top is golden and the bread bounces back when touched.
6. Allow to cool in the tin for 5 minutes before turning out onto a wire rack to cool completely before slicing.

TIP Best consumed within 3 days of baking or slice and freeze individual portions for school lunchboxes.

DATE AND BANANA LOAF

MAKES 1 LOAF (ABOUT 10 SLICES)

Dairy, egg and refined sugar free, this loaf is nearly a weekly staple at our house. Mix by hand in one bowl and set to bake. Toast it for breakfast, take it to work or put in the school lunchbox: any way you eat it, you will be wanting more.

INGREDIENTS

1 cup (160 g/5¾ oz) chopped dried pitted dates
1 cup (250 ml/9 fl oz) boiling water
2 over-ripe bananas, mashed
3 tablespoons sunflower oil
1¾ cups (260 g/9¼ oz) self-raising flour
1 teaspoon bicarbonate of soda (baking soda)

LET'S PUT IT ALL TOGETHER

1. Preheat the oven to 180°C (350°F). Line a 20 × 10-cm (8 × 4-inch) loaf tin with baking paper and set aside.
2. In a bowl, cover the dates with the boiling water and soak for 5 minutes.
3. To the soaked dates and water, add the banana, oil, flour and bicarbonate of soda and mix well to combine.
4. Pour the batter into the prepared loaf tin and bake for 40 minutes or until the bread bounces back when touched.
5. Allow to cool in the tin for 5 minutes before turning out onto a wire rack to cool completely before slicing.

  TIP Best consumed within 3 days of baking, or freeze individual portions for school lunchboxes.

ZUCCHINI, APPLE AND CARROT LOAF

MAKES 1 LOAF (ABOUT 10 SLICES)

Vegetables and fruit combine to make a deliciously moist loaf with hints of cinnamon and nutmeg. This is another loaf that is ideal toasted for breakfast or popped into the work or school lunchbox. You can peel the zucchini if your littlies are fussy about green vegetables.

INGREDIENTS

2 eggs
½ cup (125 ml/4 fl oz) sunflower oil
¾ cup (150 g/5 ½ oz) brown sugar
2 zucchini (courgettes), grated
2 Granny Smith apples, grated
1 carrot, grated
1 ½ cups (225 g/8 oz) self-raising flour
1 teaspoon bicarbonate of soda (baking soda)
1 teaspoon ground cinnamon
½ teaspoon ground nutmeg
½ cup (45 g/1 ½ oz) desiccated (dried shredded) coconut

LET'S PUT IT ALL TOGETHER

1. Preheat the oven to 170°C (325°F). Line a 20 × 10-cm (8 × 4-inch) loaf tin with baking paper and set aside.
2. In a large bowl, combine the eggs, oil and brown sugar. Whisk until smooth.

3. Add the grated zucchini, apple and carrot to the egg mixture and mix well.
4. Add all of the remaining ingredients to the bowl and stir until well combined.
5. Pour the mixture into the prepared loaf tin and bake for 45–50 minutes or until the top bounces back when touched. Allow to cool in the tin for 5 minutes before turning out onto a wire rack to cool completely before slicing.

TIP Best consumed within 3 days of baking, or freeze individual slices for school lunchboxes.

RASPBERRY AND COCONUT LOAF

MAKES 1 LOAF (ABOUT 10 SLICES)

I love the way the zingy raspberries pop in this loaf. They add colour and flavour to a delicious coconut base.

INGREDIENTS

2 eggs

½ cup (110 g/3¾ oz) caster (superfine) sugar

400 ml (14 fl oz) coconut milk

2 cups (180 g/6¼ oz) desiccated (dried shredded) coconut

1¾ cups (260 g/9¼ oz) self-raising flour

1½ cups (185 g/6½ oz) frozen raspberries

LET'S PUT IT ALL TOGETHER

1. Preheat the oven to 170°C (325°F). Line a 20 × 10-cm (8 × 4-inch) loaf tin with baking paper and set aside.

2. Put the eggs and caster sugar into a bowl and whisk to combine. Add the coconut milk, desiccated coconut and flour and stir to combine. Gently fold the raspberries through the batter. Pour into the prepared loaf tin and bake for 1½ hours or until the top bounces back when touched.

3. Allow the loaf to cool in the tin for 5 minutes before turning out onto a wire rack to cool completely before slicing.

  TIP Best consumed within 3 days of baking, or freeze individual slices for school lunchboxes.

OLD-FASHIONED CHOCOLATE SLICE

MAKES 16

Something these old-style recipes have taught me is that simple ingredients are still the best. This slice (tray bake), made with basic baking items, makes a wonderful snack in a lunchbox, at parties, for fêtes, school fundraisers, and so on.

INGREDIENTS

Base

125 g (4½ oz) butter, softened

½ cup (100 g/3½ oz) brown sugar

½ cup (45 g/1½ oz) desiccated (dried shredded) coconut

½ cup (75 g/2¾ oz) plain (all-purpose) flour

½ cup (75 g/2¾ oz) self-raising flour

2 tablespoons unsweetened cocoa powder

1 egg

Topping

1 cup (125 g/4½ oz) icing (confectioners') sugar

3 tablespoons unsweetened cocoa powder

sprinkles, for decorating

LET'S PUT IT ALL TOGETHER

1. Preheat the oven to 180°C (350°F). Line a 20-cm (8-inch) square baking tin with baking paper and set aside.
2. Put all of the ingredients for the base into a food processor and process for 30 seconds or until they start to come together.

3. Press the base into the prepared tin and bake for 20 minutes. Allow to cool completely before icing. Leave the slice in the tin you cooked it in to ice it.

4. To make the icing, sift the icing sugar and cocoa into a medium bowl. Add 1 teaspoon of water (add a little more if necessary) to make a smooth paste that is slightly runny but still thick.

5. Spread the icing over the cooled base and top with the sprinkles. The slice will set quickly in about 10 minutes in the fridge. Cut into 16 pieces.

CHOC-CHIP SLICE

MAKES 16

This recipe has a delicious caramel undertone with the chocolate chips sprinkled on top. Being such a versatile mix, you could sprinkle it with seeds, nuts, coconut, white chocolate chips, sultanas (golden raisins) or experiment with different toppings each week to keep things interesting.

INGREDIENTS

125 g (4½ oz) butter, melted
¾ cup (125 g/4½ oz) brown sugar
1 egg
1 teaspoon natural vanilla essence
1 cup (150 g/5½ oz) plain (all-purpose) flour
½ teaspoon baking powder
¼ teaspoon bicarbonate of soda (baking soda)
a pinch of salt
¾ cup (125 g/4½ oz) chocolate chips

LET'S PUT IT ALL TOGETHER

1. Preheat the oven to 180°C (350°F). Line a 20-cm (8-inch) square baking tin with baking paper and set aside.
2. In a bowl, combine the melted butter, brown sugar, egg and vanilla. Mix well to form a smooth caramel batter.
3. Add the flour, baking powder, bicarbonate of soda and salt to the batter and mix well.

4. Pour the batter into the prepared tin. Sprinkle with the chocolate chips and bake for 15–20 minutes until the top is golden and bounces back when touched.

5. Allow to cool slightly in the tin, then lift the baking paper out with the slice, transfer it to a work surface and cut into squares.

APPLE AND OAT SLICE

MAKES 20

Do you have a toddler who only eats a bite out of an apple
and abandons the rest? Or do you have some apples that
are not quite as crisp as you would like? This slice
(tray bake) is perfect for using up these unwanted apples.
Grated apple and hearty oats come together in a slice
that will give you the energy to get through the day. Try
swapping the apples for pears or half the apples for carrots.

INGREDIENTS
5 small red apples, grated
1 cup (95 g/3¼ oz) rolled (porridge) oats
¾ cup (110 g/3¾ oz) self-raising flour
1 cup (150 g/5½ oz) plain (all-purpose) flour
¼ cup (55 g/2 oz) raw (unrefined) sugar
1 teaspoon ground cinnamon
100 ml (3½ fl oz) olive oil
2 eggs

LET'S PUT IT ALL TOGETHER

1. Preheat the oven to 180°C (350°F). Line a 20-cm (8-inch) square
   baking tin with baking paper and set aside.
2. I grate the apples in my food processor to save time, but a hand
   grater will work just as well. Put the grated apples and all the dry
   ingredients into a bowl. Mix well to combine.
3. In a smaller bowl or jug, whisk together the olive oil and eggs,
   then pour them onto the dry ingredients and mix well to combine.

4. Pour the batter into the prepared tin, level off the top and bake for 25 minutes, or until the top is lightly golden and bounces back when touched.

5. Allow to cool in the tin for 5 minutes before turning out onto a wire rack to cool completely before slicing.

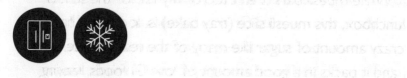

SIMPLE MUESLI SLICE

MAKES 16

While muesli bars aren't top of my list for the school lunchbox, this muesli slice (tray bake) is. It doesn't have a crazy amount of sugar like many of the ready-made bars and it packs in a good amount of low-GI foods, leaving you feeling fuller for longer and providing you with a more sustained energy level which aids in concentration. You can easily make this gluten free by using a gluten-free muesli.

INGREDIENTS

3 cups muesli (there are many varieties available, so choose one
    with a fruit and seed combination that your family likes)
½ cup (45 g/1 ½ oz) desiccated (dried shredded) coconut
3 large eggs
¼ cup (60 ml/2 fl oz) sunflower oil
¼ cup (90 g/3 ¼ oz) honey

LET'S PUT IT ALL TOGETHER

1. Preheat the oven to 180°C (350°F). Line a 20-cm (8-inch) square cake tin with baking paper and set aside.
2. Put all of the ingredients into a bowl and mix until combined. Pour into the prepared tin and bake for 30 minutes or until lightly golden on top. Allow to cool in the tin for 5 minutes before turning out onto a wire rack to cool completely before slicing.

NEAPOLITAN CAKE

MAKES 1 LOAF (ABOUT 10 SLICES)

Chocolate, pink and white all swirled together to
make a fun cake that can be used for birthdays,
or for morning or afternoon tea. It looks impressive
and doesn't require much effort.

INGREDIENTS

125 g (4½ oz) butter, softened
¾ cup (165 g/5¾ oz) sugar
1 teaspoon natural vanilla essence
2 eggs
1½ cups (225 g/8 oz) plain (all-purpose) flour
1½ teaspoons baking powder
red food colouring
¼ cup (30 g/1 oz) unsweetened cocoa powder

LET'S PUT IT ALL TOGETHER

1. Preheat the oven to 180°C (350°F). Line a 20 × 10-cm (8 × 4-inch)
   loaf tin with baking paper and set aside.

2. In the bowl of a standing electric mixer fitted with the beater
   attachment, or using a handheld electric beater, cream together
   the butter, sugar and vanilla. Add the eggs, one at a time, beating
   well after each addition.

3. Add the flour and baking powder to the egg mixture and
   beat until combined. Spoon one-third of the mixture into the
   prepared loaf tin (this is the white part).

4. Spoon half of the remaining mixture into a bowl and mix in a drop
   of red food colouring to form a pink batter. Spoon this into the tin.

5. Add the cocoa to the remaining mixture and beat until combined. Spoon this into the tin. Use a knife to swirl the three colours together.
6. Bake for 30 minutes or until the top of the cake bounces back when touched. Allow to cool in the tin for 5 minutes before turning out onto a wire rack to cool completely before slicing.

CRAZY CHOCOLATE BANANA CAKE

SERVES 12

The crazy part of this cake is that it can be made
without eggs, butter and milk and still work.
There is nothing conventional about this recipe except
the end result: a lovely moist cake that is perfect with
chocolate icing (frosting). This cake has also been
referred to as 'Depression cake' because it is very cheap
to make. It is baked in the dish that you mix it in.

INGREDIENTS

1½ cups (225 g/8 oz) self-raising flour
3 tablespoons unsweetened cocoa powder
¾ cup (165 g/5¾ oz) sugar
1 teaspoon bicarbonate of soda (baking soda)
1 teaspoon white vinegar
5 tablespoons light olive oil (or sunflower oil)
2 over-ripe bananas, mashed
1 teaspoon natural vanilla essence

LET'S PUT IT ALL TOGETHER

1. Preheat the oven to 160°C (315°F).
2. Combine the flour, cocoa, sugar and bicarbonate of soda in the
    ovenproof dish or tin that you want to bake the cake in. Make
    three indents in the dry mix.

3. In one indent, pour the vinegar; pour the oil into another; and in the last add the banana, followed by 1 cup (250 ml/9 fl oz) of water and the vanilla. Use a fork to mix all the ingredients together really well, making sure to get everything off the bottom.
4. Bake the cake for 55 minutes. Allow to cool in the dish or tin, then turn out onto a wire rack to cool completely before spreading icing on top. You will find icing recipes on page 337.

  TIP Omit the cocoa to make a delicious banana cake.

BASIC CUPCAKES TO DECORATE

MAKES 12

A basic cupcake recipe is handy to have. Cupcakes are easy to make and decorate with icing (frosting), sprinkles, fruit and so on. They are an impressive party cake for birthdays, baby showers, engagement parties and more.

INGREDIENTS

125 g (4½ oz) butter, softened
½ cup (110 g/3¾ oz) sugar
1 teaspoon natural vanilla essence
2 eggs
2 cups (300 g/10½ oz) self-raising flour
¾ cup (185 ml/6 fl oz) milk

LET'S PUT IT ALL TOGETHER

1. Preheat the oven to 180°C (350°F). Place paper muffin cases in a 12-hole standard muffin tin and set aside.

2. In the bowl of a standing electric mixer fitted with the beater attachment, or using a handheld electric beater, beat the butter, sugar and vanilla until light and creamy. Add the eggs, one at a time, beating well after each addition.

3. Add the flour and milk to the egg mixture and mix until just combined.

4. Divide the mixture evenly between the paper cases. Bake for 15–20 minutes until the cupcakes bounce back when touched. Allow to cool in the tray for 5 minutes, then transfer to a wire rack to cool completely before decorating. See page 339 for an icing recipe.

THE FLUFFIEST
CHOC-CHIP PIKELETS

MAKES ABOUT 15

I came up with this variation on a normal pikelet
(mini sweet pancake) recipe when I didn't have any
eggs left but, strangely, had two egg whites sitting
in my fridge. To my surprise the pikelets were the
fluffiest I had ever made and this is now my
go-to recipe.

INGREDIENTS

1 cup (150 g/5½ oz) self-raising flour
1 tablespoon raw (unrefined) sugar
2 egg whites
200 ml (7 fl oz) milk
1 teaspoon natural vanilla essence
butter, for frying (optional)
chocolate chips, for decoration

LET'S PUT IT ALL TOGETHER

1. Put all of the ingredients except the chocolate chips in a small
    bowl, mix well with a whisk for a good minute.
2. Heat a non-stick frying pan over medium heat. You can use a
    little butter if you like.

3. Drop tablespoon-size amounts of batter into the heated pan. Once the first side is cooked (it will form bubbles on the top), scatter with some chocolate chips, then flip and cook on the second side for 30 seconds. Repeat until all the batter is used.

  TIP The chocolate chips can be left out to make plain pikelets.

LEMONADE SCONES

MAKES ABOUT 24

If you asked me how many batches of these lemonade scones I have made I would reply with hundreds. Why that many? I used to run a café and every morning I would make a double batch of these scones to sell: sometimes I would be back in the kitchen during the mid-morning rush to get another batch in the oven because they were sold out. I have this recipe down pat: I could probably do it with my eyes shut.

INGREDIENTS

5 cups (750 g/1 lb 10 oz) self-raising flour
a pinch of salt
1 cup (250 ml/9 fl oz) thickened (whipping) cream
1½ cups (375 ml/13 fl oz) lemonade (carbonated soft drink such as Sprite or 7up)
milk, for brushing

LET'S PUT IT ALL TOGETHER

1. Preheat the oven to 200°C (400°F). Line a baking tray with baking paper and set aside.
2. Put 4 cups (600 g/1 lb 5 oz) of the flour with the salt into a large bowl. Make a well in the centre and pour in the cream followed by the lemonade. Using a butter knife, bring the mixture together to form a dough. You want to work the dough gently to make sure you get a nice rise on the scones.

3. Turn the dough out onto a floured bench. If it seems a little too sticky add ½ to 1 cup (75 g/2¾ oz) of the remaining flour. Gently press the dough out into an oval shape that is about 3 cm (1¼ inches) thick.

4. Using a circular cookie cuter or a glass, push down through the dough (don't twist) to cut out the scones. Place on the prepared tray. Repeat until all the dough is used.

5. Brush the top of the scones with some milk and bake for 10–15 minutes until they rise and have a lovely golden colour on top.

6. Delicious enjoyed warm with jam and cream or butter.

APRICOT AND CHIA SEED BLISS BALLS

MAKES APPROXIMATELY 12

Bliss balls are my go-to chocolate alternative as they
are sweet enough to curb an afternoon craving.
With no added sugar, these apricot and
chia seed balls will keep everyone happy.

INGREDIENTS

1 cup (155 g/5½ oz) dried apricots
½ cup (35 g/1¼ oz) shredded coconut, plus extra for rolling
4 tablespoons chia seeds

LET'S PUT IT ALL TOGETHER

1. Put all of the ingredients into the bowl of a food processor fitted
   with the metal chopping blade, add 1 tablespoon of water and
   process until completely broken down and the mixture starts to
   combine.
2. Roll tablespoon-size amounts of the mix into balls and then roll
   in the extra coconut. Repeat until all the mix is used.

TIP Bliss Balls last up to two weeks in the
fridge so I always double my batch.

DATE, SULTANA AND OAT BLISS BALLS

MAKES 20–24

I love experimenting with the ingredients that I have on hand. It means that I get to use up all those bits and pieces I have hanging around in the cupboard, which leads to saving money and making a new variation of an already favourite recipe. These are a great 'fake chocolate' for after dinner and perfect for the lunchbox for little and big kids.

INGREDIENTS
1 cup (160 g/5¾ oz) dates
1 cup (170 g/6 oz) sultanas (golden raisins)
¼ cup (30 g/1 oz) unsweetened cocoa powder
½ cup (95 g/3¼ oz) rolled (porridge) oats
½ cup (45 g/1½ oz) desiccated (dried shredded) coconut, plus extra for rolling

LET'S PUT IT ALL TOGETHER

1. Put the dates and sultanas into the bowl of a food processor fitted with the metal chopping blade and process for 1 minute. Add 1 tablespoon of water and process for a further 30 seconds. The mix will be slightly sticky, if not, add another tablespoon of water.
2. Add the remaining ingredients and process until it all starts to come together.
3. Take tablespoon-size amounts of the mix and roll into balls, then roll in the extra coconut. Repeat until all the mix is used.

  TIP Bliss Balls last up to two weeks in the fridge so I always double my batch.

ENERGY BITES

MAKES 12

Packed full of oats to keep you going, these are perfect to add to a lunchbox or to snack on as an afternoon pick-me-up.

INGREDIENTS

2 cups (190 g/6¾ oz) rolled (porridge) oats
½ cup (45 g/1½ oz) desiccated (dried shredded) coconut
2 tablespoons unsweetened cocoa powder
¼ cup (90 g/3¼ oz) honey
3 tablespoons melted butter (or coconut oil, or light olive oil)

LET'S PUT IT ALL TOGETHER

1. Put the rolled oats, coconut and cocoa into a food processor fitted with the metal chopping blade and process until the oats are broken down.
2. With the food processor running, add the honey and melted butter. Process until combined. Stop the processor and test the mixture by pressing a small amount together with your hands; the mixture should stay clumped together. If it doesn't, return it to the processor and add a little bit more honey.
3. Press into moulds (you can use silicone moulds or an icetray with a flexible base), or spread onto a tray approximately 5 mm (¼ inch) thick.
4. Set in the fridge for 1 hour.
5. Once set, remove from the moulds and store in an airtight container in the fridge.

  TIP They will last up to two weeks in the fridge.

CORN RELISH DIP TWO WAYS

MAKES APPROXIMATELY 10 SERVES

This is such a simple dip, served with bread, crackers or carrot sticks. It takes just three ingredients and a minute to put together.

INGREDIENTS

250 g (8 oz) light cream cheese
125 g (4 oz) corn relish
2 teaspoons vegetable stock powder

LET'S PUT IT ALL TOGETHER

1. Put all of the ingredients in a food processor fitted with the plastic mixing blade and process until smooth. For a bit more texture, fold through some extra corn relish.

VARIATION Replace the cream cheese with 1 cup (245 g/8¾ oz) light sour cream. No need to process, just stir it all together and then fold through 1 cup (100 g/3½ oz) grated cheddar cheese.

WARM CREAMY BACON AND CHEESE DIP

SERVES 12+

The bacon flavour dominates the creamy mix, but then when you dip into it you get a surprise with the stringy mozzarella grabbing onto the carrot stick, making you just want to get it into your mouth.

INGREDIENTS

6 rindless bacon rashers (such as D'Orsogna Premium Short Cut), chopped
125 g (4½ oz) light cream cheese
1¼ cups (310 g/11 oz) light sour cream
1 cup (125 g/4½ oz) grated mozzarella cheese
1 spring onion (scallion), white part only, finely chopped
thinly sliced vegetable sticks, broccoli florets or crackers, to serve

LET'S PUT IT ALL TOGETHER

1. Preheat the oven to 200°C (400°F). Cook the bacon in a hot frying pan until just crunchy.
2. In a bowl, combine the cooked bacon with the cream cheese, sour cream, half the mozzarella cheese and the spring onion and mix well. Spoon into an ovenproof dish, then top with the remaining cheese.
3. Bake for 20 minutes or until the cheese is golden on top and the dip is warmed through.
4. Serve with vegie sticks, broccoli or crackers.

TIP Best eaten on the day of making.

ROASTED PUMPKIN, SPINACH AND PINE NUT DIP

MAKES APPROXIMATELY 4 SERVES

This dip is super-healthy and also super-delish: your guests will be coming back for more.

INGREDIENTS

½ butternut pumpkin (squash), unpeeled
2 garlic cloves, peeled
3 tablespoons olive oil
50 g (1¾ oz) pine nuts
a small handful of baby spinach leaves, finely chopped
1 basil leaf, finely chopped

LET'S PUT IT ALL TOGETHER

1. Wrap the pumpkin in foil with the garlic cloves and 1 tablespoon of olive oil. Seal the foil and bake in a preheated 200°C (400°F) oven for 20 minutes or until soft.
2. Scrape the pumpkin flesh from the skin and put it in a bowl along with the garlic. Chill in the fridge.
3. Heat the pine nuts in a small frying pan over medium heat, stirring constantly until they start to brown, then remove from heat. Roughly chop the toasted pine nuts.
4. Once the pumpkin mixture has cooled, add the chopped pine nuts and the remaining ingredients and mix well to combine.
5. Serve with crackers, corn chips or carrot sticks.

 TIP Store in an airtight container in the fridge.

AVOCADO HUMMUS

Cheap and easy to make, this dip will become a favourite in no time. It's great for snacking on in the afternoon, in the school lunchbox or for toddlers, who always love to dip. Swap vegetable sticks for softer dipping options for little ones with fewer teeth.

INGREDIENTS

400 g (14 oz) tin chickpeas (garbanzo beans), drained and rinsed
1 ripe avocado
2 tablespoons hulled tahini
juice of ½ lemon
1 garlic clove, finely chopped
2 tablespoons olive oil

LET'S PUT IT ALL TOGETHER

1. Put all of the ingredients into the bowl of a food processor fitted with the metal chopping blade and process until well combined. You may need to scrape the side down as you go.
2. Serve the hummus with vegetable sticks or pita bread.

 TIP Store in an airtight container in the fridge.

Bits 'n' Pieces

From icing (frosting) to stuffing these are the
little extras that can help complete a dish.

FOOD-PROCESSOR STUFFING

MAKES ENOUGH FOR 1 CHICKEN

When roasting a chicken, I love to make my own stuffing. It's cheaper, tastes better and is satisfying to make. Bread that is a few days old works best, as does frozen bread.

INGREDIENTS

4 slices bread
1 garlic clove, peeled
1 teaspoon finely grated lemon zest
1 teaspoon chicken stock powder
3 tablespoons chopped fresh parsley

LET'S PUT IT ALL TOGETHER

1. Put all of the ingredients into the bowl of a food processor fitted with the metal chopping blade. Season with salt and pepper and process until broken down to a fine crumb.
2. Add 3 tablespoons of water and continue to process until the stuffing comes together.
3. Remove the stuffing from the food processor and stuff into the chicken.

TIP If you don't have a food processor, freeze the bread and use a grater to shred it, then mix with the other ingredients.

TACO SEASONING

Full of ground herbs and spices and with no thickening agents added, you can also tailor the taste of your taco seasoning to suit what your family likes. Make a large batch for the same price as a couple of serves of ready-made seasoning and you'll also have the satisfaction of making something yourself.

INGREDIENTS

1 teaspoon garlic powder

1 teaspoon dried oregano

1 teaspoon sweet paprika

3 teaspoons ground cumin

2 teaspoons salt

2 teaspoons freshly ground black pepper

1 teaspoon chilli powder

LET'S PUT IT ALL TOGETHER

1. Simply combine all of the ingredients in a bowl and mix well. Double or triple the recipe and store in an airtight jar in the pantry ready for your next Mexican night.

 TIP Pre-made taco seasoning will last as long as normal dried herbs do.

HIDDEN VEGETABLE TOMATO SAUCE

MAKES ABOUT 1 LITRE/35 FL OZ

This is one of my favourite sneaky dishes. I always make it when I feel that the family isn't getting enough vegetables in their diet. It hides a mountain of vegies and tastes great. Use it as a pizza sauce, pour it over pasta or cook meatballs in it.

INGREDIENTS

¼ head of cauliflower, finely chopped
¼ head of broccoli, finely chopped
1 carrot, grated
1 zucchini (courgette), grated
3 cups (750 ml/26 fl oz) tomato passata
your favourite herbs, to taste
3 garlic cloves, peeled
2 teaspoons sugar

LET'S PUT IT ALL TOGETHER

1. In a large saucepan, put all of the vegetables, cover them with water and boil, uncovered, for about 20 minutes until they are soft.
2. Add the passata, herbs, garlic and sugar and season with pepper, then reduce to a simmer and cook for 1 hour.
3. Remove from the heat and allow to cool slightly.
4. Use a stick blender or a food processor and process until smooth.

GARLIC AND HERB BREAD

SERVES 4–6

My homemade garlic bread only requires a single spread of this herb and garlic butter. It comes out full of flavour, not full of dripping butter.

INGREDIENTS

100 g (3½ oz) butter, softened
2 garlic cloves, finely chopped
1 tablespoon fresh flat-leaf (Italian) parsley, finely chopped
4–6 bread rolls of your choice (bread that is a few days old works well)

LET'S PUT IT ALL TOGETHER

1. In a bowl, place the softened butter (if it is still hard, simply grate the butter into the bowl), garlic, parsley and a sprinkling of salt. Mix well until it is all evenly combined.
2. Spread a layer of the herb and garlic butter onto the bread (sliced in half lengthways) and either bake at 200°C (400°F) or cook under the grill (broiler) for 5–10 minutes until it just starts to turn golden brown.

TIP Any leftover herb and garlic butter can be wrapped in plastic wrap and popped into a resealable plastic bag and frozen for next time. When I am ready to use it again, I simply cut slices off (once softened).

BASIL AND CASHEW PESTO

MAKES APPROXIMATELY 1 CUP

This pesto has a lovely mild, sweet flavour from the cashews instead of the traditional pine nuts, which makes it very family friendly when added to a meal. Use it to toss through pasta, marinate chicken skewers or serve as a dip.

INGREDIENTS

2 large handfuls of fresh basil
1 small handful of raw cashews
¼ cup (60 ml/2 fl oz) olive oil
a squeeze of lemon juice
75 g (2¾ oz) parmesan cheese, roughly chopped

LET'S PUT IT ALL TOGETHER

1. Put all of the ingredients into a food processor fitted with the metal chopping blade. Season with salt and pepper and process until everything is really well combined and chopped up.

TIP Store in a sterilised jar topped with extra olive oil in the fridge for 5–7 days. Alternatively, divide it into the compartments of an icetray and freeze.

WRAPS

Have you ever gone to the freezer to check if you had some back-up bread to make sandwiches for lunch and found the cupboard bare? Never fear; I'm going to show you how easy it is to make your own wraps.

INGREDIENTS

2 cups (300 g/10½ oz) plain (all-purpose) flour
1 teaspoon baking powder
1 teaspoon salt
1 tablespoon olive oil, plus extra for cooking

LET'S PUT IT ALL TOGETHER

1. Put all of the ingredients into a large bowl, add 1 cup (250 ml/ 9 fl oz) of water and use a butter knife to stir them until they form a smooth ball.
2. Divide the dough evenly into four balls. Roll each ball out until it is 1 mm (1/32 inch) thick.
3. Lightly oil a frying pan and heat over low heat. Lay one round of bread in the pan and cook until it starts to lightly brown on one side, then flip it over and cook the other side. If any air bubbles form, simply prick them with a fork.

TIP Best eaten on the day they are made.

YOGHURT FLATBREAD

MAKES 6

This yoghurt flatbread sounds like it shouldn't work but it does. Two ingredients and some extra flavouring will give you bread to enjoy with a curry, use as a pizza base or simply for dipping.

INGREDIENTS

1 cup (150 g/5½ oz) self-raising flour
1 cup (260 g/9¼ oz) plain yoghurt
a pinch of salt
1 tablespoon dried herbs and spices (optional)
olive oil, for cooking

LET'S PUT IT ALL TOGETHER

1. Put all of the ingredients into a bowl (including the herbs and spices, if using) and use a butter knife to bring the dough together.
2. Turn the dough out onto a floured work surface and knead until a ball forms. Divide the dough into six portions.
3. Using a flour-dusted rolling pin, roll each portion out to a 2-mm (1/16-inch) thick circle. Repeat until all the dough is rolled.
4. Heat a tablespoon of olive oil in a large non-stick frying pan, then cook the bread until golden on both sides. Repeat for the remaining flatbreads.

TIP Best eaten on the day they are made.

BUTTERCREAM ICING

MAKES ENOUGH FOR ONE 20-CM
(8-INCH) ROUND CAKE—DOUBLE OR TRIPLE THE
INGREDIENTS TO MAKE A LARGER BATCH

This is my go-to birthday cake icing (frosting). It is easy to make and easy to work with. It sets hard when the cake is in the fridge and then softens as it comes to room temperature.

INGREDIENTS

125 g (4½ oz) butter, softened
1½ cup (330 g/11¾ oz) icing (confectioners') sugar
1 teaspoon natural vanilla essence
1 tablespoon milk

Variations

Chocolate: add ¼ cup (30 g/1 oz) unsweetened cocoa powder
Coloured: add 1 drop of food colouring (vary depending on colour you want to achieve)

LET'S PUT IT ALL TOGETHER

1. Put the butter and icing sugar into the bowl of a standing electric mixer fitted with the beater attachment, or use a handheld electric beater, and beat until light and creamy.
2. Add the vanilla, milk and any variations to the bowl and continue to beat until combined.
3. Spoon and spread the icing onto a completely cooled cake or cupcake. You can also use a piping (icing) bag to make fancier decorations.

TIP It is important that the butter is at room temperature otherwise you won't get a lovely creamy icing.

ROYAL ICING

Don't be fooled by the runny consistency of this icing
when you make it, because it sets hard. Use it for
decorating biscuits.

INGREDIENTS

1 egg white
1 teaspoon lemon juice
2 cups (250 g/9 oz) icing (confectioners') sugar, sifted
drops of food colouring (optional)

LET'S PUT IT ALL TOGETHER

1. In a large bowl, whisk together the egg white and lemon juice.
   Gradually add the sifted icing sugar and continue to mix until a
   smooth paste is formed.
2. If you want to colour the icing, simply divide the base mixture
   into small bowls and then add drops of your chosen colours and
   mix through.
3. I like to spoon the icing into resealable plastic bags, clip off one
   of the corners and use this as a piping (icing) bag to pipe the
   icing onto the biscuits.

NOTE The icing will set quickly, so make sure you use it as soon
as you make it.

CUPCAKE GLAZE

This is such an easy way to decorate cupcakes, you don't need any piping (icing) skills. Add sprinkles and you will have pretty cupcakes in no time.

INGREDIENTS
2 cups (250 g/9 oz) icing (confectioners') sugar, sifted
2 tablespoons milk
drops of food colouring

LET'S PUT IT ALL TOGETHER

1. Put all of the ingredients into a bowl and mix until a smooth paste is formed.
2. Drizzle and spread onto the top of cooled cupcakes.

TIP Add 1 drop of food colouring to make a coloured glaze.

Reader Recipes

Cooking For Busy Mums readers have submitted their families' favourite recipes to share with yours. Here's a selection.

MANGO AND APPLE BIRCHER MUESLI

BY DINIELLE FARQUHARSON

SERVES 1

Bircher museli makes a great start to the day. You can make it the night before and wake up to a delicious and nutritious breakfast that will keep you going well into the morning. This serves one but you can simply double or triple the recipe and keep in the fridge for up to 3 days.

INGREDIENTS

⅓ cup (35 g/1¼ oz) rolled (porridge) oats
½ cup (130 g/4½ oz) plain yoghurt
½ apple, grated or finely chopped
¼ teaspoon ground cinnamon
1 tablespoon chopped walnuts, or other nuts or seeds
1 mango cheek, diced
honey, to serve (optional)

LET'S PUT IT ALL TOGETHER

1. Mix the oats, yoghurt, apple, cinnamon and walnuts in a container and leave overnight in the fridge to soak. Put the mango on top when you serve and add a drizzle of honey (if using).

TIP You can simply combine the mango with the rest of the ingredients if you prefer, before you put it in the fridge.

CHICKEN AND MUSHROOM RISOTTO

BY SALLY AMOS

SERVES 4

....

A family favourite, especially with my two year olds and
three year olds. This recipe makes enough for hubby
to take to work the next day too.

....

INGREDIENTS

¼ cup (60 ml/2 fl oz) olive oil

250 g (9 oz) boneless, skinless chicken thigh fillets, cut into 5-mm
(¼-inch) thick pieces

100 g (3½ oz) mushrooms, cut into 5-mm (¼-inch) thick pieces

2 tablespoons crushed garlic

1 tablespoon butter

1 onion, finely chopped

2 cups (440 g/15½ oz) arborio rice

1 teaspoon dried thyme (or oregano)

¼ cup (60 ml/2 fl oz) dry white wine (such as chardonnay)

5 cups (1.25 litres/44 fl oz) chicken stock

¾ cup (80 g/2¾ oz) finely grated parmesan cheese, plus extra
to serve

LET'S PUT IT ALL TOGETHER

1. Heat 2 tablespoons of olive oil in a frying pan over low to medium heat. Add the chicken and cook until it starts to brown. Then add the mushroom and garlic, stir and cook for about 5 minutes. Remove from the heat and set aside while you cook the rice.
2. Meanwhile, heat the butter and the remaining olive oil in a large saucepan over medium heat. Add the onion and cook, stirring, for 5 minutes until soft and translucent. Add the rice and dried thyme. Cook, stirring, for about 1 minute until the rice appears slightly 'glassy'.
3. Pour the wine into the pan and cook until the liquid is absorbed. Stir in the stock, about ½ a cup (125 ml/4 fl oz) at a time, and stir until the liquid is absorbed. Repeat until all of the stock is used (this will take about 20 minutes or so).
4. Add the chicken mixture and parmesan cheese to the rice. Stir through and serve immediately. Tastes great seasoned with salt and pepper, a sprinkling of parmesan cheese and even spinach leaves on top.

BEEF CASSEROLE

BY SILE O'DRISCOLL

SERVES 4–6

The perfect dinner to warm you up during winter.
Budget and family friendly.

INGREDIENTS

900 g (2 lb) stewing steak (chuck steak), diced
olive oil, for frying
1 onion
1 garlic clove, chopped
300 g (10½ oz) mushrooms, quartered
1 celery stalk, chopped
300 ml (10½ fl oz) red wine
425 ml (15 fl oz) beef stock
400 g (14 oz) tin diced tomatoes
fresh or dried mixed herbs, to taste
cooked rice or mashed potato, to serve

LET'S PUT IT ALL TOGETHER

1. Preheat the oven to 220°C (425°F).
2. In a large frying pan over medium–high heat, brown the steak in a splash of oil and transfer to a casserole dish. In the same pan, fry the onion, garlic and mushrooms and add to the casserole dish when they are soft.

3. Add the celery, red wine, stock, tomatoes, herbs and salt and pepper to the mixture in the casserole dish, cover with the lid and bake for 20 minutes. Turn the heat down to 180°C (350°F) and continue cooking for 90 minutes or until the meat is tender.
4. Serve with rice or mashed potato.

CHICKEN AND RICE CASSEROLE

BY MEGAN LOVELL

SERVES 4–6

I love this recipe because it takes about 5 minutes to prepare, then I can leave it to bake while I organise the kids. Everyone loves it, even the baby, for whom I pop a small amount in the blender and whizz it up.

INGREDIENTS

420 g (15 oz) tin condensed cream of chicken soup
1 cup (200 g/7 oz) basmati rice
1.5–2 kg (3 lb 5 oz–4 lb 8 oz) chicken drumsticks
1½ cups (150 g/5½ oz) frozen mixed vegetables

LET'S PUT IT ALL TOGETHER

1. Preheat the oven to 180°C (350°F).
2. Empty the tin of soup into a large casserole dish, fill the empty tin with water and add it to the soup, then whisk to combine.
3. Pour the rice evenly over the liquid.
4. Lay the drumsticks in a row in the casserole dish and scatter the frozen vegetables around the drumsticks, filling in the gaps. Season with salt and pepper (you can also add any other seasoning you like, such as dried herbs: thyme is really nice).
5. Bake uncovered for 45 minutes to 1 hour until the chicken flesh bounces back when touched.

ONE-DISH CURRIED PORK CUTLETS

BY MICHELLE PETERS

SERVES 4

Turn ordinary pork cutlets into a flavour-packed baked dinner.

INGREDIENTS

2 tablespoons curry powder

4 pork cutlets

olive oil, for frying

225 g (8 oz) tin pineapple slices in juice

220 g (7¾ oz) tin mushrooms in butter sauce

1 teaspoon butter

1 cup (250 ml/9 fl oz) cooking cream

2 vegetable stock cubes

1 tablespoon cornflour (cornstarch)

cooked rice, to serve

LET'S PUT IT ALL TOGETHER

1. Preheat the oven to 200°C (400°F).
2. Mix 1 tablespoon of curry powder with salt and pepper and sprinkle over the pork to cover completely. Heat a little olive oil in a large non-stick frying pan over medium–high heat and fry the pork until golden brown on each side. Transfer to an ovenproof dish.
3. Drain the pineapple and mushrooms and save the juices for later.

4. Fry the pineapple rings in the same frying pan you used for the pork, until they start to brown and caramelise (about 5 minutes). Lay them on top of the cutlets.
5. Fry the mushrooms in the same pan for 5 minutes. Layer the mushrooms on top on the pineapple.
6. Reduce the heat to medium and add the butter and the remaining curry powder to the pan, stirring for 1 minute. Add the reserved juices from the tins, the cooking cream and stock cubes and stir until combined. Bring the sauce to the boil, then reduce to a simmer. Thicken the sauce by mixing the cornflour with 2 tablespoons of water. Stir a small amount into the pan at a time and bring back to the boil. Pour the sauce over the meat and toppings.
7. Bake the curried pork cutlets for 40–50 minutes. Serve with rice.

EASY MANGO CURRIED CHICKEN

BY TAMSIN ALLEN

SERVES 4–6

A deliciously easy one-dish dinner that will have the family coming back for seconds.

INGREDIENTS

2 tablespoons olive oil

2 onions, chopped

500 g (1 lb 2 oz) boneless, skinless chicken thigh fillets, diced

2 tablespoons curry powder

1 tablespoon plain (all-purpose) flour

400 g (14 oz) tin mango slices in juice

2 tablespoons chicken stock powder

400 ml (14 fl oz) tin light coconut milk or low-fat cream

cooked rice, to serve

LET'S PUT IT ALL TOGETHER

1. Heat the oil in a large non-stick frying pan over medium heat.
2. Add the onion and sauté.
3. Add the chicken and cook, stirring, until lightly browned.
4. Stir in the curry powder and flour, cooking for about 1 minute.
5. Drain the mango, reserving the flesh and putting the juice into a jug or bowl.
6. Mix the stock powder with the mango juice and add to the chicken in the frying pan. Bring to the boil, stirring constantly.

7. Combine the reserved mango with the coconut milk or cream, add it to the chicken mixture and cook for a further 10 minutes or so until thickened.
8. Serve with rice.

BASIL CHILLI PRAWN LINGUINE

BY COLLEEN WILSON

SERVES 2

A fresh and easy pasta dish that is on the table in no time.
If serving to little ones, simply add the chilli after serving.

INGREDIENTS

150 g (5½ oz) linguine
2 tablespoons olive oil
1 teaspoon crushed garlic
1 small red chilli, thinly sliced
150 g (5½ oz) peeled and deveined raw prawns
12 basil leaves, shredded
¼ cup (30 g/¼ oz) coarsely grated parmesan cheese
½ lime

LET'S PUT IT ALL TOGETHER

1. Bring a large saucepan of water to the boil. Add the linguine and cook for 8 minutes. Drain.
2. While the pasta is cooking, heat 1 teaspoon of olive oil in a large non-stick frying pan, add the garlic and chilli and cook for 1 minute.
3. Add the prawns to the pan and cook for a further 3–4 minutes until the prawns are opaque. Toss the cooked pasta with the prawn mixture in the frying pan. Add the basil and the remaining oil and toss until heated through. Add the parmesan cheese, then season with salt and pepper and a squeeze of the lime before serving.

TACO SALAD

BY MEGAN LOVELL

SERVES 4–6

I serve my kids the salad with meat on top and corn chips on the side of their plate, plus a bit of sour cream to dip. I make a layered stack on my own plate (chips, salad, meat, cheese, dips) and my husband likes to just pile it all up and smash his corn chips over it. This is a healthy Mexican dinner alternative, as you focus on the salad and only have the corn chips as a small side.
Great for Taco Tuesday!

INGREDIENTS

½ iceberg lettuce
1 red (Spanish) onion, sliced
1 red capsicum (pepper), sliced
2 tomatoes, sliced
1 avocado
500 g (1 lb 2 oz) minced (ground) beef or boneless, skinless chicken thigh fillets, chopped
olive oil, for cooking
1 quantity Taco Seasoning (see page 331)
175 g (6 oz) corn chips
1 cup (100 g/3½ oz) grated tasty cheddar cheese
250 g (9 oz) sour cream
150 g tomato salsa

LET'S PUT IT ALL TOGETHER

1. Prepare and layer the lettuce, onion, capsicum, tomato and avocado in a large serving dish, then refrigerate until dinner. I often make this earlier in the day if I know that after school is going to be busy.
2. Brown the mince or fully cook the chicken with some oil in a large non-stick frying pan. Add the taco seasoning and set aside. To get the seasoning to adhere to the mince or chicken, add ¼ cup (60 ml/2 fl oz) of water.
3. Serve the meat in the frying pan, the salad in the serving dish and the corn chips in a bowl. Add the grated cheese, sour cream and salsa as each person likes.

TIP Sometimes I serve this with corn cobs, or I mix tinned corn in with the salad.

SUPER-TASTY MEATLOAF

BY HELEN LAWRENCE

SERVES 4–6

This meatloaf has hidden vegies for the kids, sausage mince so that it is cheap, and zucchini to keep it moist and tasty. I sometimes make these in cupcake cases and top with pumpkin and sweet potato mash.

INGREDIENTS

300 g (10½ oz) sausage mince (or any kind of ground meat)
1 zucchini (courgette), grated
1 carrot, grated
1 egg
½ cup (55 g/2 oz) dry breadcrumbs
2 tablespoons tomato sauce (ketchup)
1 tablespoon mixed dried herbs
olive oil spray

LET'S PUT IT ALL TOGETHER

1. Preheat the oven to 180°C (350°F).
2. Mix the sausage mince, zucchini and carrot together in a large bowl.
3. Add the remaining ingredients to the bowl and combine with your hands until an even consistency is reached.
4. Spray a 24 × 10-cm (9½ × 4-inch) loaf tin with olive oil and fill with the meatloaf mixture.
5. Bake the meatloaf for 45 minutes or until it comes away from the edges of the tin.
6. Allow to cool slightly in the tin before removing and slicing to serve.

JAPANESE CHICKEN BITES

BY HELEN LAWRENCE

SERVES 4

I never manage to make enough of these bites for my husband. Serve with steamed vegies and rice and cover with yummy teriyaki sauce.

INGREDIENTS

4 boneless, skinless chicken thigh fillets, cut into bite-size pieces
¼ cup (60 ml/2 fl oz) soy sauce (low sodium)
I tablespoon finely grated fresh ginger
cornflour (cornstarch), to coat chicken
sunflower oil, for frying

LET'S PUT IT ALL TOGETHER

1. Put the chicken in a container with an airtight lid and cover with the soy sauce and ginger. Close the lid and shake until all of the chicken is coated evenly. Leave in the fridge for a minimum of 4 hours (can be prepared before work and it will be ready to use in time for dinner).
2. Spread the cornflour on a plate and coat some of the marinated chicken. Dust off any excess.
3. In a frying pan or wok, heat some oil and fry the coated chicken, in batches, until golden brown. Repeat until all the chicken is cooked.
4. Drain the chicken on paper towel and serve immediately.

WARM POTATO SALAD

BY HELEN LAWRENCE

....

Perfect to take to a barbecue or serve as a side dish.

....

INGREDIENTS

500 g (1 lb 2 oz) baby potatoes, cut in half
½ cup (75 g/2¾ oz) chopped rindless bacon
1 spring onion (scallion), finely chopped
½ cup (50 g/1¾ oz) grated parmesan cheese
½ cup (125 g/4½ oz) sour cream
1 teaspoon Moroccan seasoning

LET'S PUT IT ALL TOGETHER

1. Place the potatoes in a microwave-safe container and fill with water to cover. Cook the potatoes in the microwave for 8–10 mins until tender, drain and cool slightly.
2. Cook the bacon and spring onion in a non-stick frying pan until golden brown.
3. Add all of the ingredients to the potatoes and stir until combined. Season with salt and pepper to taste. Transfer to a salad bowl to serve.

WORLD'S EASIEST RASPBERRY TART

BY MICHELLE PETERS

SERVES 6

With only a handful of ingredients you will have this tart made in no time and everyone asking for seconds.

INGREDIENTS

2 eggs
160 g (5¾ oz) caster sugar
100 g (3½ oz) plain (all-purpose) flour
1½ tablespoons butter
300 g (10½ oz) frozen raspberries
ice cream or whipped cream, to serve

LET'S PUT IT ALL TOGETHER

1. Preheat the oven to 200°C (400°F).
2. Using a standing electric mixer fitted with the beater attachment, beat the eggs and sugar together until light and fluffy. Add the flour a little at a time. Beat until combined.
3. Grease the base and side of an ovenproof dish with 1 teaspoon of butter.
4. Pour the batter into the prepared dish and scatter the frozen berries on top.
5. Dot the remaining butter randomly on top of the tart. Bake for 35–40 minutes until golden and set.
6. Serve warm with ice cream or whipped cream.

DELICIOUS NO-BAKE CHEESECAKE

BY KENDALL BROWN

I love this recipe because there isn't too much to clean up, there's no gelatine to work with and there's no baking! You can omit the lime juice and change it up a little . . . get creative!

INGREDIENTS

200 g (7 oz) plain biscuits (I use Butternut Snap Cookies)
110 g (3¾ oz) unsalted butter, melted
400 g (14 oz) tin sweetened condensed milk
400 g (14 oz) cream cheese, at room temperature
2 teaspoons natural vanilla essence
⅓ cup (80 ml/2½ fl oz) lime juice (or use lemon, if you like)

LET'S PUT IT ALL TOGETHER

1. Crush the biscuits to a fine crumb in a food processor or using a rolling pin. Mix with the melted butter.
2. Line a 20-cm (8-inch) springform cake tin with baking paper and firmly press the biscuit mixture in to form a base, then refrigerate while preparing the filling.
3. In a standing electric mixer fitted with the beater attachment, combine the condensed milk, cream cheese and vanilla and beat on medium–high speed until smooth. Add the lime (or lemon) juice and beat on high speed until thick and smooth.
4. Pour the cheesecake mixture over the base and chill in the fridge until set (at least 6 hours, but preferably overnight).

TIPS Add some caramel to the cheesecake mixture
Use chocolate ripple biscuits (cookies) for the base
Add cocoa to the cheesecake mixture
Add passionfruit pulp and mango slices to the cheese-
cake mixture
The possibilities are endless!

Index